Innovative
Indian Cuisine

Supriya Nabar

Dedication

This book is dedicated to my children Kunal and Yamini for their honest opinions about the recipes and suggestions some of which were incorporated in the book and my husband Prafulla without whose support this book would not be published. Also this book is dedicated to millions of people who have an adventurous spirit to try something new and unknown.

Contents

Soups and Dals

Appetizers

Salads and Vegetables

Eggs

Chicken

Lamb

Fish and Shellfish

Breads and Rice Dishes

Sweet Little Things

Introduction

Indian cookery has a wide range of delicacies. Every state has a different cuisine. Some recipes have been forgotten and lost in time. Others have evolved, keeping up with modern lifestyles. In the modern world, through exposure to different cultures, we have begun to mimic the western world in order to suit our hectic lifestyles and satisfy our palates.

In this book, my quest has been to choose recipes that are simple and easy to prepare so that any novice will be able to cook them with ease. The idea of this book is not to make Indian cooking complicated, but to simplify it so that it can be done in easy steps. At the same time, it is modified to give it a modern twist.

The idea is to make the recipes healthy and nutritious so that they can be custom fitted into our modern lifestyles. People want to eat healthy, nutritious, and tasty meals, but at the same time do not want to devote too much time to slogging in their kitchens. My idea with this cookbook is to take complicated recipes and reinvent them so that they keep their nutritious value and provide visually appealing, satisfying, and delicious dishes.

The recipes make use of herbs and spices used not only in Indian cooking, but also in other cultures; yet the basic foundation of the cookbook is Indian. I believe that no one can teach you to cook, but rather, you should devise your own way of cooking. You should use a cookbook to act as a guide, and the quantities of the main ingredients can be modified to suit your own taste.

I hope recipes such as Egg-Spinach Fritters, Spicy Salmon Cakes, Eggplant-Tomato Bake, Cinnamon Chicken, and Vanilla Vermicelli Pudding tempt you enough to try these recipes and incorporate them into your life.

Soups and Dals

In Indian cooking, soups are not served as a first course. Traditional Indian meals are served with all the courses together on a single plate. However, there are Indian soups that are served on occasion. These soups could be simple vegetarian fare, or they might be meat-based or seafood-based. They can be hot and spicy or cold and refreshing—especially in the summer. Lentils and beans are almost always eaten with rice and bread and are popular elements in Indian cuisine.

Chilled Mango Soup

serves 4   *calories per serving: 196*   *total fat per serving: 0.2 g*

Mangoes in Indian cuisine are cooked as a vegetable or eaten as a dessert. Here, canned mango puree is substituted for fresh, and converted into a soup. The addition of coconut milk gives it a somewhat exotic flavor with ginger, green chili, and a little hint of salt and pepper. The sensations of sweet, hot, and spicy play on the tongue at different times, making for a sublime experience. This recipe can be served before a meal or as a dessert; it will definitely start or end the meal with elegance.

Ingredients

1 large can mango puree
1 13.5 fl. oz. can coconut milk
¼ teaspoon saffron threads, soaked in milk
1 Thai bird chili
1 teaspoon grated ginger
¼ teaspoon garam masala
Salt and pepper to taste
½ cup cilantro leaves, washed and finely chopped

Method

In a large saucepan, combine the mango puree, coconut milk, and soaked saffron threads. Cook the mixture for about 5 minutes. Add the Thai chili, ginger, garam masala, salt, and pepper. Cool the mango-coconut milk puree and put it in the refrigerator for 1 to 2 hours.

To serve, remove the cold mango soup from the fridge and garnish with cilantro leaves

Spinach Soup with Roasted Garlic

serves 4   calories per serving: 417   total fat per serving: 20.7 g

Spinach is a popular vegetable in Indian cooking, because leafy greens are found in abundance, and because it is considered to be nutritious and high in calcium. Here, the sweetness of roasted garlic combines with and enhances the flavor of spinach, especially when paired with a few crunchy fried shrimp on top as a garnish. This is a good winter or spring soup.

Ingredients

1 whole head garlic
1 Tablespoons olive oil
½ pound shrimp, peeled and deveined
4 cups fresh spinach leaves, washed and finely chopped
1 green jalapeño chili, minced
1 medium-sized red onion, peeled and sliced thinly
1 teaspoon cumin powder
¼ teaspoon cayenne pepper
½ teaspoon garam masala
4 cups chicken or vegetable broth
1 teaspoon light cream
1 Tablespoon olive oil
Salt and pepper to taste

Method

Roast the garlic in a preheated, 325-degree oven for 45 minutes. Add a few drops of olive oil and rub salt and pepper on the garlic before you put it in the oven for roasting. Cut the garlic in half and separate and peel the garlic cloves.

In a large saucepan, heat the olive oil and add the spinach, green chili, red onion, cumin powder, cayenne pepper, and garam masala. Cook for 6–10 minutes over medium heat. Next, add the chicken or vegetable broth. Simmer for 20 minutes, and then puree the spinach-broth mixture in a food processor or grinder. Pan fry the shrimp in a few teaspoons of oil until crisp but not tough.

Ladle the soup into individual bowls. To serve, garnish with a few roasted garlic cloves and some sautéed shrimp. Add salt and pepper to taste.

Spicy Pumpkin Soup

serves 4   *calories per serving: 410*   *total fat per serving: 26.7 g*

Pumpkin soup is a fall dish. It resembles the fall colors and can be very warming when the weather gets cold. Here, pumpkin pairs with coconut milk, ginger, nutmeg, and cayenne to give it a spicy sweetness.

Ingredients

1 Tablespoon canola oil
1 yellow onion, peeled and minced
1 carrot, peeled and sliced thinly
1 stalk celery, thinly sliced
2 teaspoons grated ginger
2 cans pumpkin pulp
½ teaspoon cumin powder
1 can coconut milk
1 pint chicken broth
½ teaspoon nutmeg
A pinch of cayenne pepper
Salt and pepper to taste

Method

In a large pot, add canola oil, onion, carrot, celery, and ginger. Let this cook for a few minutes. Add pumpkin pulp, cumin, coconut milk, and chicken broth. Let this mixture simmer for 10 minutes. Add nutmeg and a pinch of cayenne pepper, and cook for 2 minutes more.

Garnish with cilantro leaves and serve.

Asparagus Soup with Spinach

serves 4   *calories per serving: 122*   *total fat per serving: 5.5 g*

This spring soup is a unification of two green vegetables. The crunchy texture of asparagus and the sponginess of spinach come together to make a soup that is not only tasty, but also has a wonderful green color.

Ingredients

1 Tablespoon canola oil
1 bunch asparagus, washed and cut into bite-size pieces
1 bunch baby spinach
1 green jalapeño chili, deseeded and finely chopped
2 shallots, peeled and chopped finely
1 bay leaf
½ teaspoon cumin powder
¼ teaspoon cayenne pepper
2 cloves garlic, peeled and chopped finely
4 cups chicken broth
½ cup cilantro leaves, washed and chopped coarsely
1 Tablespoon light cream
½ teaspoon garam masala
Salt and pepper to taste

Method

In a large Dutch oven, add oil and sauté the asparagus, baby spinach, chili, shallots, bay leaf, cumin powder, cayenne pepper, and garlic. Let this cook for 5 minutes. Add the broth and cilantro and cook for 5 minutes.

Let the broth come down to room temperature and discard the bay leaf. Blend mixture to pulverize into soup.

Transfer the soup back into the pot and simmer for 5 minutes. Add cream just before you serve the soup. Add garam masala and salt and pepper to taste. Serve hot.

Cold Cucumber Soup

serves 4   *calories per serving: 80*   *total fat per serving: 1.5 g*

Cucumber soup is a summer favorite and is supposed to be eaten cold. The light-green color of cucumber interspersed with yogurt and garnished with dill makes for a soup that's pleasing to look at and to eat.

Ingredients

2 English cucumbers, deseeded and grated (discard the water)
1 large jalapeño chili, deseeded and minced
½ cup dill leaves, chopped finely (keep some aside for garnish)
½ cup scallions, chopped finely (keep some aside for garnish)
1 cup yogurt, thinned with water to a viscous consistency
Salt and pepper to taste

Method

In a blender, combine cucumbers, jalapeño chili, dill, and scallions. To this mixture, add yogurt and blend well.
Put it in a large bowl and chill thoroughly. Add remaining dill and scallions for garnish. Add salt and pepper to taste.

Fisherman's Soup

serves 4   calories per serving: 151   total fat per serving: 4.7 g

This is a basic seafood recipe where seafood is added to give it a fishy flavor and enhance its protein value. You can add the seafood of your choice. This is a colorful soup and can be served as a main course with some nice crusty bread and a salad.

Ingredients

12 medium-sized tomatoes, peeled and cut into cubes (save any juice)
4 Tablespoons yellow or orange lentils
2 Tablespoons canola oil
1 cup medium-sized shrimp, peeled and deveined
1 cup mussels, cleaned and bearded
2 medium-sized shallots, peeled and chopped finely
1 teaspoon mustard seeds
¾ teaspoon asafetida
8–10 curry leaves
1 lemongrass stalk
1 teaspoon tamarind paste
3 cups chicken or seafood broth
3 Tablespoons rasam powder
1 Tablespoon ground black pepper
1 cup cilantro leaves, finely chopped
Salt and pepper to taste

Method

Puree the tomatoes, pass through a sieve, and set aside. Cook the lentils in small amounts of water for 30 minutes or until the lentils are soft and some water is remaining.

In a large Dutch oven, pour the canola oil and then add the cooked lentils, shrimp, mussels, shallots, mustard seeds, asafetida, curry leaves, lemongrass, and tamarind paste. Fry this for a few minutes.

Add broth and tomatoes and let it simmer until it comes to a boil. Add salt to taste. Add rasam powder, black pepper, and cilantro leaves, and serve piping hot.

Spicy Lentils

serves 4   calories per serving: 359   total fat per serving: 10.6 g

Lentils are supposed to be eaten with rice, but they can also be served as a soup. Lentils are naturally rather bland, but with the help of spices they are elevated to a higher level. In this recipe, the intermingling of spices produces varied exotic flavors.

Ingredients

2 Tablespoons canola oil
2 cups boiled lentils
1 bay leaf
3 cloves garlic, peeled and sliced very thinly
3 large tomatoes, chopped coarsely
2 dried red chilies, broken into pieces
½ teaspoon brown sugar
1 teaspoon turmeric
4 cups water
1 teaspoon clarified butter
1 teaspoon cumin seeds
1 teaspoon kasuri methi
½ teaspoon asafetida
8–10 curry leaves
3 Tablespoons lemon juice
3 Tablespoons cilantro leaves
1 teaspoon garam masala
1 teaspoon sesame oil
Salt to taste

Method

Boil the lentils in ample amounts of water until they are cooked, about 30 to 40 minutes, and set aside.

In a large wok, heat oil to sizzling. Add the bay leaf, garlic, tomatoes, red chilies, brown sugar, and turmeric. Sauté this for 2–3 minutes until the tomatoes and spices are well blended. Add water and let simmer for 8–10 minutes. Add lentils to the garlic-tomato mixture.

In another small pot, add the clarified butter. To this, add the cumin seeds, kasuri methi, asafetida, and curry leaves. Let this sizzle for a minute or so and add this to the lentils. Top it with lemon juice, cilantro leaves, garam masala, and sesame oil. Add salt to taste. Serve hot.

Three-Bean Curry

serves 4   calories per serving: 304   total fat per serving: 5.0 g

Three-bean curry is a medley of different beans. Here, red beans, black beans, and adzuki beans are combined together to make a curry. The beans are of different colors and sizes, thus providing a range of texture and flavor.

Ingredients

1 Tablespoon canola oil
¾ cup dried red beans, rinsed 2–3 times
1 cup dried black beans, rinsed 2–3 times
1 cup dried adzuki beans, rinsed 2–3 times
2 medium-sized tomatoes, finely chopped
1 Tablespoon ginger, finely minced
1 teaspoon garlic, finely chopped
1 medium-sized onion, finely chopped
2 dried red chilies
½ teaspoon turmeric powder
½ teaspoon cumin seeds
½ teaspoon cumin powder
1 teaspoon ground coriander
1 teaspoon dried fenugreek leaves
1 teaspoon dried mint leaves
3–4 kokum pods
1 teaspoon brown sugar
6 curry leaves
1 cup cilantro leaves, washed and chopped finely
Salt to taste

Method

Soak the dried beans overnight; then cook the beans in a pot with water for 1 hour or until soft. Pour oil in a medium-sized vessel. Next, add tomatoes, ginger, garlic, onion, red chilies, turmeric powder, cumin seeds, cumin powder, ground coriander, dried fenugreek leaves, mint leaves, kokum pods, brown sugar, and curry leaves. Sauté this mixture for 3 to 4 minutes. Add the beans to the pot and let it cook for 4 minutes. Add water if it looks too thick in consistency.

Add salt and cilantro leaves at the end and serve hot.

Spring Vegetable Soup

serves 4   *calories per serving: 171*   *total fat per serving: 8.2 g*

This is a simple vegetable soup with different vegetables added to the pot. The addition of coriander powder, cumin powder, and garam masala add pungency to the soup, and the coconut milk tones down the spiciness. It is a hearty soup, great for serving on a cold winter night.

Ingredients

2 Tablespoons canola oil
2 cups frozen corn kernels, defrosted
1 red bell pepper, chopped into small pieces
1 cup frozen green peas
2 medium-sized carrots, cubed
1 green chili, thinly sliced
½ teaspoon cumin powder
½ teaspoon ground coriander
½ teaspoon garam masala
2 cups vegetable stock
1 can coconut milk
1 Tablespoon lime juice
¼ teaspoon sugar
3 Tablespoons cilantro leaves
Salt to taste

Method

In a large saucepan, pour the canola oil. Add the corn, red bell pepper, green peas, and carrots. Sauté the vegetables until they are caramelized.

To this mixture, add the green chili, cumin, coriander, and garam masala. Add vegetable stock and coconut milk. If the soup becomes too thick, add some water or stock. Let the vegetable soup boil gently so that the vegetables get cooked. Remove the pan from the heat and add lime juice, sugar, and salt. Garnish with cilantro leaves.

Sweet and Sour Tamarind Broth

serves 4–6   calories per serving: 94   *total fat per serving: 5.8 g*

This soup is basically a broth that is flavored with tamarind. Tamarind is often used in Indian cooking to impart a sour element. To make it more nutritious, Swiss chard and chickpeas are added.

Ingredients

2 Tablespoons canola oil
1 one-inch piece of ginger, peeled and chopped finely
1 teaspoon cumin seeds
5 curry leaves
3 large carrots, peeled and cut into small pieces
1 bunch Swiss chard, cut into thin strips
1 can chickpeas
4 cups vegetable or chicken broth
1 Tablespoon maple syrup
2 teaspoons tamarind paste
¼ teaspoon cayenne pepper
½ teaspoon black pepper
3 Tablespoons cilantro leaves
Salt to taste

Method

Put oil, ginger, cumin seeds, curry leaves, carrots, Swiss chard, and chickpeas in a large saucepan and sauté until vegetables are soft.

Add broth, maple syrup, tamarind paste, cayenne pepper, and

black pepper. Let the whole pot simmer at a low heat for 15 to 20 minutes.
Add salt to taste, garnish with cilantro leaves, and serve.

Appetizers

Appetizers are savory foods eaten in the morning as breakfast or as snacks with afternoon tea. They are made with vegetables, cheese, meat, or fish. Appetizers such as Shrimp Fritters with Goat Cheese and Asian Corn Fritters can also be good appetizers before your meal.

Asian Corn Fritters

serves 4   *calories per serving: 229*   *total fat per serving: 16.3 g*

Fritters can be made with vegetables, chicken, or seafood. Here, corn is mixed with cabbage, spices, and flour to make fritters. The corn and cabbage both provide the crunchiness to the fritter.

Ingredients

3 Tablespoons canola oil for frying
2 cups frozen corn
1 cup cabbage, shredded into thin strips
½ cup and a few Tablespoons all-purpose flour
1 medium-sized onion, minced
1 teaspoon ground coriander
½ teaspoon cumin powder
½ teaspoon garam masala
1 cup cilantro leaves, washed and chopped finely
1 large egg, lightly beaten
1 teaspoon grated ginger
2 garlic cloves, peeled and minced
1 jalapeño chili pepper, minced
Salt and pepper to taste

Method

In a bowl, combine all ingredients except oil. Mix gently and add more flour if mixture does not bind.

In a shallow fry pan, pour canola oil. Using a spoon, gently ladle the corn mixture into the oil. The fritters should be the size of a golf ball. Flip them and fry the fritters on the other side. When they turn golden brown, remove the fritters from the oil and serve hot.

Herb Potato Pancakes

serves 4–6   calories per serving: 198   *total fat per serving: 2.6 g*

Potato pancakes are an integral part of every culture. Here, the humble potato has the fortune to mix with the herbs, where it gets elevated to a different level. Potato pancakes are served as a snack or can be served as a side dish in a meal.

Ingredients

1 pound Yukon Gold potatoes, boiled in their skins and cooled
2 large eggs, lightly beaten
2 scallions, chopped finely
1 teaspoon cumin powder
1 teaspoon ground coriander
½ cup cilantro leaves, chopped finely
½ cup oregano leaves, chopped finely
½ cup all-purpose flour
1 jalapeño, seeded and deveined
1 lemon, cut and juiced
3 Tablespoons canola oil for frying
Salt to taste

Method

Peel the potatoes and mash them in a large bowl. Add the eggs, scallions, cumin, coriander, cilantro leaves, oregano leaves, flour, jalapeño pepper, and lemon juice. Mix well, divide the mixture into balls, and flatten them.

Take each flattened ball and give it a round shape.
Fry the pancakes until light brown, flipping occasionally to
ensure they brown on both sides. Serve hot with chutney.

Spicy Salmon Cakes

serves 4   *calories per serving: 660*   *Total fat serving: 16.0 g*

Salmon is ubiquitous in Indian cuisine, and can be used in many different dishes. Here, salmon is mixed with herbs and spices, and the salmon takes on their flavors. Any other fatty fish, such as mackerel or bluefish, can be used.

Ingredients

½ pound salmon fillet
2 cups hot chicken broth
4 large Yukon Gold potatoes
1 Tablespoon light cream
½ cup dill leaves
1 cup parsley leaves
1 jalapeño chili, chopped finely
2 cloves garlic, chopped finely
1 teaspoon ginger, minced finely
1 teaspoon Dijon mustard
½ teaspoon chaat masala
1 teaspoon garam masala
Salt and pepper to taste
1 cup all-purpose flour
2 large eggs, beaten lightly
2 cups panko bread crumbs
3 Tablespoons canola oil
4 Tablespoons lemon juice

Method

Poach the salmon in hot broth for 6 minutes; then remove the salmon and let it cool.

Boil the potatoes; test to make sure they are soft. Drain the water and let the potatoes cool. Peel and mash them in a large bowl, using a masher. Using a fork, flake the salmon into bite-size pieces. Add the flaked salmon to the potato mixture and add cream. Blend this salmon-potato mixture well.

Add the dill leaves, parsley, jalapeño, garlic, ginger, Dijon mustard, chaat masala, garam masala, salt, and pepper.

Make into balls and flatten these balls. Dip them into the flour, then into the egg, and lastly transfer into the panko bread crumbs.

Pan-fry the salmon cakes and drain the oil. Add a bit of salt and pepper to the cakes. Sprinkle them with lemon juice and serve hot.

Cheesy Shrimp Fritters

serves 4–6   calories per serving: 299   total fat per serving: 4.3 g

Fritters are served as appetizers or as little tidbits before the main course. Here, shrimp is filled with goat cheese and fried. The sweetness of shrimp is mixed with the tanginess of the goat cheese in a burst of flavors.

Ingredients

1 pound of shrimp, peeled, deveined, and slit open
¼ teaspoon cayenne pepper
1 teaspoon turmeric powder
2 Tablespoons lime juice
Salt to taste
1 medium-sized log of goat cheese, about 4 oz.
2 Tablespoons canola oil

Ingredients for Batter

1 cup of chickpea flour
¼ teaspoon baking soda
Salt to taste
½ cup cold water
¼ teaspoon cayenne pepper

Method

Marinate the cleaned, deveined shrimp with cayenne pepper, turmeric powder, and lime juice. Add a very tiny amount of salt and let the shrimp sit in this marinade for 1 hour.

Next, mix chickpea flour, salt, baking soda, and cold water in a bowl. Whisk the ingredients. If the batter becomes too thick, add more water a teaspoon at a time to attain the right consistency. If it becomes too thin, add some chickpea flour one teaspoon at a time to the mixture.

Take the shrimp out of the marinade and fill them with goat cheese. Set aside until ready to be fried.

In a small pan-like vessel, pour 2 Tablespoons of oil, and let the oil heat up. Gently insert the shrimp into the oil and fry. When they turn golden brown on both sides, remove them, drain on a paper towel, and serve hot.

Egg-Spinach Fritters

serves 4   *calories per serving: 128*   *total fat per serving: 11.1 g*

Spinach fritters are a favorite. In this recipe, spinach is paired with boiled eggs to create a slightly different but tasty fritter. These fritters have a reasonable amount of protein and are delicious.

Ingredients

4 medium-sized organic eggs
½ cup cilantro leaves
3 or 4 scallions, washed and chopped finely
1 cup spinach leaves, cleaned and chopped finely
½ teaspoon cayenne pepper
½ teaspoon turmeric powder
½ teaspoon smoked paprika
½ teaspoon chaat masala
½ teaspoon cumin seeds
½ teaspoon kasuri methi leaves
A few teaspoons of water
½ teaspoon salt
5 Tablespoons of chickpea flour
1 teaspoon baking soda
3 Tablespoons canola oil for deep-frying

Method

Boil the eggs in water until they are done, about 10 minutes. Immerse the eggs in an ice bath. Then transfer the eggs into another bowl and carefully remove the eggshells. Chop the eggs coarsely.

Chop the cilantro leaves, scallions, and spinach leaves, and transfer this, as well as the eggs, into a large bowl.

Add cayenne pepper, turmeric powder, smoked paprika, chaat masala, cumin seeds, kasuri methi, and salt to taste.

Add chickpea flour, baking soda, and a few teaspoons of water to the bowl, and mix the ingredients until well blended.

In a medium-sized, shallow frying pan, immerse Tablespoon of the mixture in hot oil. When the fritters turn golden-brown, transfer them to a platter lined with paper towels.

Sprinkle it with some coarse salt and chaat masala and serve hot.

Exotic Shrimp Patties

serves 4   *calories per serving: 327*   *total fat per serving: 22.6 g*

Patties can be made in many different ways; shrimp is minced finely and then mixed with different flavorings to make patties. Since shrimp has a sweet taste of its own, it can easily take the essence of the spices and blend well to make delicate little patties. This can be served as a side dish in a meal or as an appetizer.

Ingredients

3 Tablespoons canola oil

1 pound medium-sized shrimp, cleaned and chopped

½ cup thinly sliced scallions

¼ cup mint leaves, chopped finely

½ cup cilantro leaves, chopped finely

½ teaspoon chili powder

2 teaspoons ginger, peeled and minced

2 cloves garlic, peeled and minced

¼ teaspoon asafetida

A pinch of sugar

Salt to taste

1 teaspoon baking powder

2 Tablespoons rice flour and 3 Tablespoons chickpea flour, combined

3 tablespoons lemon juice or lime juice

Method

In a large bowl, combine chopped shrimp, scallions, mint leaves, cilantro leaves, chili powder, ginger, garlic, asafetida, sugar, and salt. Add the baking powder and flour mixture. Mix the batter well.

With the stove on medium, heat the oil and then add the shrimp fritters. Fry the fritters until golden-brown for about 2 minutes or less. The shrimp should turn translucent.

Drain the fritters on the paper towel, sprinkle them with lemon juice and coarse salt, and serve hot.

Sweet Potato and Carrot Patties

serves 4–6   calories per serving: 136   total fat per serving: 11.9 g

Sweet potato and carrot are both sweetish in taste. They are combined here to produce a sweet patty that is tinged with chili and other spices to create a balance of flavors. Potatoes or other root vegetables can be substituted to create a number of variations.

Ingredients

3 large sweet potatoes
2 large carrots, peeled and sliced into chunks
2 cloves garlic, peeled and chopped finely
½ teaspoon turmeric powder
1 green chili, thinly sliced
1 teaspoon garam masala
1 Tablespoon lemon juice
1 large egg
3 Tablespoons cilantro leaves
1 slice of bread, soaked in warm water and squeezed
1 teaspoon orange zest
Salt to taste
3 Tablespoons canola for frying

Method

Set the oven at 350 degrees and roast the sweet potatoes and carrots for 25–30 minutes.

Put them in a large bowl and mash with a masher. Add garlic, turmeric, green chili, garam masala, lemon juice, egg, cilantro leaves, bread, orange zest, and salt. Mix this all together. Coat your hands with a layer of oil and start making patties. Set aside in the refrigerator to chill for 30 minutes. In a large pan, pour 3 Tablespoons of the oil. Insert a few patties at a time in a single layer. Pan-fry until one side is golden. Flip and cook the other side until cooked. Serve hot.

Crispy Zucchini Pancakes

serves 4   *calories per serving: 152*   *total fat per serving: 13.3 g*

In this dish, zucchini is grated and mixed with peanuts to form delicious pancakes. Zucchini is available throughout the year, but you can also make the pancakes with potatoes, carrots, or parsnips.

Ingredients

5 Tablespoons canola oil
1 large red onion, peeled and chopped finely
2 large cloves of garlic
4 large scallions, chopped finely
3 large zucchini, ends removed, grated
2 large eggs, beaten
1 teaspoon garam masala
¼ teaspoon cayenne pepper
½ cup unsalted peanuts, crushed into coarse powder
2–3 Tablespoons lemon juice
Salt to taste

Method

In a sauté pan, pour 1 Tablespoon oil and sauté the onion, garlic, and scallions. When this mixture cools, transfer it to another bowl and add the grated zucchini, eggs, garam masala, cayenne pepper, unsalted crushed peanuts, lemon juice, and salt.

Mix thoroughly and make small pancakes. Set them aside. In a large frying pan, add 4-5 Tablespoons oil and start adding a few zucchini pancakes at a time. Let the pancakes cook on one side, and then flip onto the other side until golden brown.

Salads and Vegetables

Salads and vegetables are side dishes and act as an accompaniment to the meal. Salads are colorful and made of vegetables, aromatic herbs, and exotic spices, along with fruits, nuts, chili peppers, and yogurt. Vegetables are served as an accompaniment to other dishes. On many occasions, vegetables and salads are used to complement the main dish. If the main dish is spicy, the salads or vegetables are mild, and vice versa.

Spinach Salad with Fritters

serves 4   *calories per serving: 263*   *total fat per serving: 21.3 g*

Spinach Salad with Fritters gives a different take on salad, because the salad is combined with crunchy, tasty fritters. Every bite has a different surprise with an assortment of vegetables for the fritters, as well as vegetables in the salad. The salad and the fritters can be stored separately so that the fritters do not lose their crunchiness. They can be combined just before serving.

Ingredients

1 packet baby spinach, washed and spun dry
1 large cucumber, peeled and cut into slices
2 medium tomatoes cut into slices
10 small florets of cauliflower,
1 green bell pepper, cut into longish strips
½ cup parmesan cheese slivers
3 Tablespoons canola oil
2 teaspoons lemon juice
Salt and pepper to taste

Ingredients for Batter

5 Tablespoons chickpea flour mixed with a few Tablespoons of water
2 Tablespoons rice flour
½ teaspoon cayenne pepper
½ teaspoon chaat masala
½ teaspoon onion seeds

1 teaspoon baking powder
½ teaspoon fennel seeds
½ teaspoon salt

Ingredients for Vinaigrette

1 Tablespoons lemon juice
3 Tablespoons olive oil
1 clove garlic, peeled and minced
½ teaspoon chaat masala

Method

Assemble the vinaigrette and set it aside.

On a big platter, lay the baby spinach leaves, cucumber, and tomato slices.

Make the batter and dip the cauliflower florets and green pepper pieces into the batter. Pan-fry them a few at a time. As you remove them from the oil, place them on a clean paper towel to drain.

Keep the fritters separated from the salad until just before serving. Add the vinaigrette to the salad, toss, and serve with the fritters in the center and the tossed salad surrounding it. Add Parmesan cheese slivers, lemon juice, olive oil, salt, and pepper to taste.

Creamy Avocado Salad

serves 4   *calories per serving: 86*   *total fat per serving: 7.0 g*

This is a salad with a few basic ingredients tossed together. The salad has unique combinations of vegetables, like avocado and radishes. The addition of sesame seeds adds a crunch and a different flavor to the succulent vegetables.

Ingredients

3 ripe Haas avocados, peeled and diced
1 large red onion, peeled and sliced thinly
1 medium-sized cucumber, peeled, seeded, and chopped into small cubes
2 tomatoes, seeded and diced
6 red radishes, cut and diced
1 jalapeño pepper, minced
Salt and pepper to taste
2 Tablespoons lemon juice
2 Tablespoons grapeseed oil
1 cup mint leaves, chopped finely
2 teaspoons white sesame seeds

Method

Cut all the vegetables and dump them in a large bowl.
Season it with salt and pepper. Add lemon juice and grapeseed oil.
Garnish it with mint leaves and toasted white sesame seeds, and serve.

Simple Mango Salad

serves 4   *calories per serving: 174*   *total fat per serving: 2.4 g*

Mango is used widely in Indian cooking. Here, it comes in the form of a simple salad that can be enjoyed in hot summer months. The sour taste of dried mango powder counteracts the sweetness of mango and creates a wonderful balance. Serve this salad cold. Pineapples or peaches can be used in place of mangoes.

Ingredients

4 mangoes, peeled and chopped into cubes
1 head of butter lettuce torn into medium-sized pieces
1 red onion chopped finely
3 green scallions, chopped finely
1 cup basil leaves cut into thin strips
1 teaspoon chaat masala
½ teaspoon mango powder
Salt and pepper to taste

Ingredients for Vinaigrette

2 Tablespoons lemon juice
¼ cup mango juice
½ cup olive oil
Salt and pepper to taste

Method

Mix all the salad ingredients in a bowl. Make the vinaigrette and pour over the salad. Gently toss the salad. Refrigerate and serve it cold.

Potato-Cucumber Salad

serves 4   calories per serving: 108   total fat per serving: 2.4 g

Potato and cucumber together in a salad is an unusual combination. The cucumber and potato with yogurt and dill leaves makes a wonderful salad. If you do not like dill leaves, you can mix it with mint leaves.

Ingredients

1 pound new potatoes, thinly sliced into rounds
1 English cucumber
½ cup red or white onion, thinly sliced into slivers
1 teaspoon chaat masala
¼ teaspoon red chili powder
2 Tablespoons fresh dill, finely chopped
2 cups plain nonfat yogurt
Salt and pepper to taste
2 Tablespoons olive oil
1 teaspoon mustard seeds
6 curry leaves

Method

Boil the potatoes in a saucepan with water; add a generous pinch of salt and let the potatoes cook until tender.
Cut the cucumber into paper-thin rounds and place them in a bowl.
To the bowl add chopped onions, chaat masala, boiled potatoes, red chili powder, chopped dill, nonfat yogurt, salt, and pepper.

In a small frying pan, pour oil, and when the oil sizzles, add mustard seeds and curry leaves. Serve cold.

Eggplant-Potato-Cheese Stacks

serves 4   calories per serving: 159   total fat per serving: 8.4 g

Pan-fried eggplant slices and potato slices are stacked along with cheese and baked in the oven. The result is a napoleon-like packet that you can serve as a side dish. This is a baked dish, so it is less labor-intensive.

Ingredients

1 pound Yukon gold potatoes, boiled for 10 minutes
1 pound eggplant, small variety, pan-fried in a little oil
2 Tablespoons canola oil
1 jalapeño pepper, stemmed, seeded, and chopped finely
1 large onion, peeled and minced
1 teaspoon minced garlic
1 teaspoon minced ginger
1 teaspoon cumin powder
1 teaspoon garam masala
Slices of cheese of your liking
1 cup cilantro leaves, chopped finely
2 Tablespoons lime juice
Salt to taste

Method

Slice the potatoes into thick rounds. Also cut eggplant into similar shapes. Keep the skin on both the potatoes and the eggplant.

In a large pot, add oil, jalapeño pepper, onion, garlic, ginger, and cumin powder and garam masala.

Mix this garnish equally among eggplant and potato. Now start stacking the potato, eggplant, and slice of cheese. Now add another layer of potato, eggplant, and cheese. Bake these packets in a hot oven at 325 degrees for 20 to 25 minutes. Garnish it with cilantro leaves and lime juice, and salt to taste.

Tomato Salad with Yogurt Cheese

serves 4   calories per serving: 82   total fat per serving: 6.9 g

Tomatoes of two different colors are combined with cumin and chaat masala and different herbs to create a simple, colorful salad. The addition of cheese at the end adds another dimension to the salad. Here, yogurt cheese is used because it has fewer calories, but you could substitute any cheese of your liking.

Ingredients

2 large red tomatoes, sliced into good-sized rounds
2 large yellow tomatoes, sliced into good-sized rounds
1 small packet of farmer's yogurt cheese
1 teaspoon cumin seeds
1 teaspoon chaat masala
Salt and pepper to taste
2 Tablespoons thyme leaves, chopped
2 cloves garlic, chopped and minced finely
2 Tablespoons olive oil
1 Tablespoon lemon juice
2 Tablespoons parsley and cilantro leaves, cleaned and chopped coarsely

Method

Arrange the tomato slices. Cut the yogurt cheese into cubes and add it to the platter. Sprinkle cumin seeds and chaat masala on the tomatoes. Add salt and pepper.

In a small jar, combine thyme leaves, garlic, olive oil, and

lemon juice, as well as salt and pepper. Pour the vinaigrette over the tomatoes and cheese.
Garnish it with cilantro and parsley leaves.

Eggplant-Tomato Bake

serves 4   *calories per serving: 82*   *total fat per serving: 7.0 g*

Eggplant has a very smoky flavor when it is cooked in the oven, and, combined with the juiciness of the tomatoes, it makes for a very earthy dish. The allspice berries with ricotta cheese make for a wonderful baked side dish.

Ingredients

2 Tablespoons olive oil
2 large eggplants
3 tomatoes, deseeded and chopped coarsely
2 cloves of garlic, peeled and chopped finely
1 teaspoon allspice berries
½ teaspoon cumin powder
1 teaspoon coriander powder
1 green jalapeño chili, minced finely
2 Tablespoons fresh cilantro leaves
2 Tablespoons fresh mint leaves, chopped coarsely
3 tablespoons lemon juice
1 cup low fat ricotta cheese
Salt and pepper to taste

Method

Brush the eggplants and tomatoes with oil and cook them in a 350-degree oven for 45 minutes.
Remove the vegetables from the oven when they're in a soft-cooked state. Add garlic, allspice berries, jalapeño, cumin, and coriander powder.

Mash the vegetables and cook them in the oven for 20 minutes or so.

Garnish the baked eggplant and tomato with cilantro, mint, lemon juice, and salt and pepper. Top it with ricotta cheese and bake for another 8 minutes.

Spicy Eggplant Medley

serves 4   calories per serving: 108   total fat per serving: 11.5 g

This eggplant salad is served as a pulpy medley. Cook the eggplant the day before so that the flavors are allowed to blend with the eggplant and it actually tastes better the next day. The lemon juice is allowed to blend with the spices and the eggplant, and together it creates a heavenly flavor in your mouth.

Ingredients

2 Tablespoons canola oil (for oiling the eggplants before grilling)
6–8 Asian eggplants
3 cloves garlic, chopped finely
½ teaspoon red chili flakes
½ teaspoon cumin powder
½ teaspoon coriander powder
½ teaspoon garam masala
1 jalapeño pepper
1 teaspoon sesame oil
2 Tablespoons olive oil
2 Tablespoons lemon juice
1 cup cilantro leaves, chopped and minced
Salt to taste

Method

Oil and grill the eggplants. Remove them from the grill. Transfer the eggplants into a bowl and mash them. Add garlic, chili flakes, cumin, coriander, and garam masala.

Chop the jalapeño pepper, garlic, and add sesame oil. Make vinaigrette of lemon juice and olive oil. Add all this to the eggplant salad. Garnish it with cilantro leaves and serve at room temperature.

Quick Cauliflower Vegetable

serves 4   calories per serving: 80   total fat per serving: 7.0 g

This is the simplest cauliflower dish. Cauliflower florets are mixed with chili and cumin seeds and then topped with cilantro leaves and lemon juice. The result is a quick and delicious side dish.

Ingredients

2 Tablespoons olive oil
1 teaspoon red chili flakes
1 teaspoon cumin seeds
1 cauliflower head, separated into florets and soaked in cold water
1 Tablespoon lemon juice
½ cup cilantro leaves
Salt to taste

Method

In a large pan, pour oil, red chili flakes, and cumin seeds.
Now add the cauliflower florets and salt.
Stir-fry the cauliflower and add lemon juice and cilantro leaves as a garnish.

Innovative Indian Cuisine

Lemony Shredded Okra

serves 4   *calories per serving: 148*   *total fat per serving: 7.4 g*

Okra is a popular vegetable in India and is commonly found in Indian meals. However, it has a slippery texture, and people love it or hate it. Here, the dried mango powder removes the sliminess of the okra, and the shredding makes the okra crispy. In India, it is often cooked with a lot of oil. In this dish, less oil is used, and lemon is used to bring in the flavor.

Ingredients

1 pound okra
2 Tablespoons canola oil
2 large onions, finely chopped
2 large garlic cloves, minced finely
2 large tomatoes, chopped finely
2 Tablespoons lemon juice
1 teaspoon lemon zest
½ teaspoon mango powder
½ teaspoon garam masala
½ cup cilantro leaves
Salt and pepper to taste

Method

Shred the okra in a food processor. Keep aside. In a large saucepan, pour oil; add onions, garlic, tomatoes and okra. Let this cook for 10 minutes on low heat. Add lemon juice, lemon zest, mango powder, and garam masala. Salt and pepper to taste. Garnish it with cilantro leaves and serve.

Root Vegetables Roast

serves 4   *calories per serving: 40*   *total fat per serving: 3 g*

Roasted vegetables are not common in Indian cooking, but various combinations of vegetables are cooked in a wok. In this recipe, the vegetables are cooked in the oven and garnished with oil, spices, and herbs. Basil is used here, but any green herb can be used for variation.

Ingredients

1 celery root
2 sweet potatoes
2 onions, thinly sliced
1 butternut squash
2 carrots
2 Tablespoons olive oil
2–3 sprigs of thyme
1 teaspoon cumin powder
½ teaspoon cayenne pepper
1 teaspoon kasuri methi
1 Tablespoon of garam masala
20 basil leaves, chopped finely
Salt and pepper to taste

Method

Roast the vegetables with oil, thyme, cumin powder, cayenne pepper, kasuri methi, and garam masala in an oven until done. Add chopped basil leaves, salt, and pepper. Stir, and serve hot.

Baked New Potatoes

serves 4   calories per serving: 222   total fat per serving: 7.1 g

In this recipe, potatoes are baked instead of being cooked in a pan with oil. This dish is easy to prepare, and since it is made in the oven it is not time-consuming or labor-intensive. Dried oregano and dill seeds, in combination with other spices, give this dish a great aroma when it comes out of the oven.

Ingredients

2 Tablespoons olive oil
2 pounds new potatoes, cut into halves
1 teaspoon paprika
¼ teaspoon chili powder
¼ teaspoon turmeric powder
½ teaspoon dried oregano leaves
½ teaspoon dill seeds
1 teaspoon coriander powder
½ teaspoon clove powder
3 Tablespoons lemon juice
2 Tablespoons cilantro leaves
Salt and pepper to taste

Method

Combine the oil and the potatoes in the baking pan and add the lemon juice and all the spices, including salt and pepper. Bake the potatoes at 350 degrees for 30 minutes or until the potatoes are cooked.

Add 2 Tablespoons cilantro leaves as garnish.

Snappy Pickled Potatoes

serves 4   *calories per serving: 168*   *total fat per serving: 7.3 g*

Potatoes are combined with pickle masala to create a very simple and tasty dish. The spiciness of the pickle masala and the tartness of the lemon juice create a balanced background in which the potatoes mingle with each other. This is a simple dish which can be made in a snap.

Ingredients

1 pound Yukon Gold potatoes, boiled in their skins
2 Tablespoons canola oil
10 curry leaves
1 teaspoon mustard seeds
½ teaspoon turmeric powder
1 teaspoon pickle masala
2 Tablespoons cilantro leaves, washed and minced
2 teaspoons lemon juice
Salt to taste

Method

Remove the boiled potatoes and let them cool. Peel them, and cut them into big chunks.

In a large wok-like vessel, pour canola oil. To this add curry leaves, mustard seeds, and turmeric powder. Let this cook for a minute or so.

Add the potato chunks and let them cook in the oil until they are well blended with the spices, about 10 minutes.

Add the pickle masala, cilantro, and lemon juice as a garnish. Salt to taste, and serve hot.

Gingered Sweet Potato

serves 4   *calories per serving: 89*   *total fat per serving: 6.8 g*

This is a sweet potato mash with undertones of ginger. The hint of nutmeg and the aromatic orange zest give it a sweetish flavor. This dish has a nice color and makes a nice side dish with any grilled meat or fish.

Ingredients

1 Tablespoon canola oil
4 sweet potatoes, peeled and roughly chopped
2 Tablespoons light cream
1 cup milk
Salt to taste
½ teaspoon nutmeg
1 Tablespoon cumin powder
2 teaspoons orange zest
½ teaspoon coriander powder
3 garlic cloves, peeled and cut into small pieces
2 shallots, peeled and minced
1 large piece of ginger, minced finely
1 Tablespoon unsalted butter

Method

Fill a large saucepan with water almost up to the brim. Add sweet potatoes and let boil for about 30 minutes. Pierce with a fork and check if they are done. Let cool slightly. Peel the sweet potatoes and mash slightly.

In a large steel bowl, combine the potatoes, cream, and milk, and mash thoroughly.

Add salt, nutmeg, cumin powder, orange zest, and coriander powder to the mashed potatoes.

In a frying pan, combine oil, garlic, shallots, ginger, and butter. Let this cook until it turns golden. Add this to the mashed sweet potatoes. Add pepper to taste.

Mix everything very well and serve hot.

Potato and Spinach Salad

serves 4   *calories per serving: 323*   *total fat per serving: 7.6 g*

Potatoes and spinach combine here to make an unusual salad. There are lots of dishes with potatoes and spinach, and this is a take on those, with the red pepper and tomato vinaigrette adding a different dimension.

Ingredients

6 medium-sized potatoes, coarsely chopped
1 bunch baby spinach leaves, coarsely chopped
Salt and pepper to taste

Ingredients for Vinaigrette

4 roasted red peppers from a jar
1 tomato, chopped
½ teaspoon cumin powder
1 teaspoon chaat masala
2 Tablespoons olive oil
1 Tablespoon apple cider vinegar

Method

In a mixer, combine 4 roasted red peppers, 1 chopped tomato, cumin powder, chaat masala, vinegar, and olive oil. Grind the whole mixture and set aside.

Place the potatoes in a pot with water and bring them to boil. Cook until tender. In a large bowl, toss the spinach and vinaigrette, add the potatoes, and season with salt and pepper.

Innovative Indian Cuisine

Stuffed Red Peppers

serves 4   *calories per serving: 110*   *total fat per serving: 4.4 g*

Stuffed peppers are a common dish in many cultures. Here, a spicy and sweet mixture is created to fill up the peppers, and later whole peppers are baked in the oven. It makes a fabulous side dish and also is easy to make.

Ingredients

4 large red peppers
1½ cups bread crumbs
1 Tablespoon olive oil
2 cloves garlic, peeled and minced
½ cup cilantro leaves, washed and minced finely
½ cup basil leaves, washed and chopped finely
1 teaspoon garam masala
1 teaspoon mango powder
1 small tomato, core removed and chopped finely
1½ cups of shredded yogurt cheese
2 Tablespoons lemon juice
Salt and pepper to taste

Method

Only the stem and cap of the pepper should be removed. Cut the pepper in half so that there are 8 halves. Lay the pepper halves on a tray. Sprinkle the peppers with 1 Tablespoon lemon juice and a little olive oil.

In another bowl, combine breadcrumbs, olive oil, garlic, cilantro, basil, garam masala, mango powder, tomato, and cheese.

Stuff this mixture into the red peppers. Bake the peppers for 40 minutes. Sprinkle with salt and pepper.

Potato Cakes with Mozzarella and Spinach Sauce

serves 4   *calories per serving: 176*   *total fat per serving: 16.3 g*

Potato cakes are basically mashed potatoes with different spices and herbs. Here mozzarella cheese is added to the mild flavor of potato cakes. The potato cakes are served with a spicy spinach sauce.

Ingredients

2 Tablespoons canola oil
5 large Yukon Gold potatoes, peeled and grated
1 medium-sized red onion
1 jalapeño pepper, deveined and minced
1 large piece of ginger, peeled and minced finely
2 cloves garlic, peeled and chopped finely
¼ cup nonfat sour cream
½ cup cilantro leaves, washed and chopped finely
½ cup scallions, washed and chopped finely
1 teaspoon garam masala
2 medium-sized eggs, beaten lightly
Salt to taste
4 ounces of buffalo mozzarella cheese

Ingredients for Spinach Sauce

1 teaspoon canola oil
1 cup spinach, washed and chopped
¼ cup frozen corn
2 cloves garlic, peeled and minced finely

½ teaspoon ginger, peeled and minced finely
½ teaspoon tomato paste
½ jalapeño pepper, washed and minced finely
1 teaspoon garam masala
1 Tablespoon light cream
Salt to taste

Method

Peel and grate the potatoes; add onion, jalapeño, ginger, garlic, sour cream, cilantro, scallions, garam masala, eggs, and salt.

Shape the pancakes and place a small piece of mozzarella cheese in the middle.

Make into small patties and fry the pancakes on either side until golden brown. Set them aside.

In a medium-sized pot, combine spinach, corn, garlic, ginger, tomato paste, jalapeño pepper, garam masala, and 4 Tablespoons of water.

Grind this mixture into a smooth consistency.

Add it in the pot along with cream and salt, and let it gently simmer. Serve the spinach sauce along with the potato cakes.

Innovative Indian Cuisine

Cottage Cheese Confetti

serves 4 *calories per serving: 240* *total fat per serving: 15.6g*

This confetti-like dish is made with colorful peppers. Paneer cheese holds well in cooking and is here combined with yogurt and cashews to make a tangy sauce in which the peppers float.

Ingredients

2 Tablespoons canola oil
1 large piece of ginger, peeled and minced finely
3 cloves of garlic, peeled and chopped finely
2 large onions, peeled and sliced thinly
1 green pepper, cored and sliced thinly
1 red pepper, cored and sliced thinly
3 large tomatoes, chopped finely
1 green chili, deseeded and chopped finely
1 teaspoon turmeric powder
1 teaspoon coriander powder
½ teaspoon cumin powder
¼ teaspoon cayenne powder
1 medium-sized slab of paneer, cut into cubes
½ cup cashews, ground into a powder
1½ cups of plain nonfat yogurt
1 teaspoon kasuri methi
½ teaspoon garam masala
½ cup chopped cilantro leaves

Method

Place the cubes of paneer in a steamer and steam it for approximately 5 minutes. Next, in a wok-like pan, drizzle the oil. Let this sizzle, and then add ginger, garlic, onions, green pepper, red pepper, tomatoes, green chili, turmeric, coriander, cumin, and cayenne powder. Let this cook for a few minutes. Stir-fry until all the vegetables are coated with oil. When the vegetables are soft, add the steamed paneer cubes.

Lower the heat and cook for a few minutes. Add powdered cashews and yogurt. Let the vegetables and paneer cook in the yogurt-cashew sauce. Add kasuri methi, garam masala, and cilantro leaves, and serve hot with bread.

Fast Cabbage Stir-Fry

serves 4   *calories per serving: 69*   *total fat per serving: 7.3 g*

This is an easy stir-fry and can be done in 15–20 minutes. It is a great side dish which requires little effort. Many vegetables are quickly stir-fried to produce a quick side dish.

Ingredients

2 Tablespoons canola oil
1 teaspoon turmeric
2 dry red chilies
1 teaspoon coriander powder
½ teaspoon cumin powder
8–10 curry leaves
1 teaspoon mustard seeds
1 medium-sized cabbage, chopped finely
Salt to taste
½ cup cilantro leaves

Method

In a wok, combine oil, turmeric, red chilies, coriander, cumin, curry leaves, mustard seeds, and chopped cabbage. Add salt and a few teaspoons of water and let it cook for a good 15 minutes.

Garnish with cilantro leaves and serve.

Eggs

Eggs are very commonly used in Indian cooking. They are eaten at breakfast in the form of omelets and scrambled eggs. Eggs can also be used in combination with vegetables like eggplant and potatoes. They are also used to make egg curries for lunch and dinner. Eggs are not commonly used to make desserts in Indian cuisine.

Scrambled Eggs with Shrimp

serves 4   *calories per serving: 177*   *total fat per serving: 12.5 g*

Scrambled eggs are universal and can be combined with spices to make a breakfast dish or a hearty bedtime snack. Also, you can use shrimp or any other meat of your choice.

Ingredients

2 tablespoons canola oil
8 large eggs
3 scallions, thinly sliced
3 cloves garlic, sliced thinly
1 teaspoon ginger, sliced thinly
1 teaspoon cumin seeds
1 jalapeño pepper, deseeded and minced finely
6 sprigs of curry leaves
1 teaspoon curry powder
1 cup small shrimp
1 cup cilantro leaves
Salt to taste

Method

In a large bowl, beat eggs until they develop a nice yellow color.

In a large pan, combine canola oil, scallions, garlic, ginger, cumin seeds, jalapeño pepper, curry leaves, and curry powder. Add shrimp and let it cook for a few minutes.

Now add eggs and scramble everything for 3–4 minutes. Remove from heat. Garnish with cilantro leaves and serve.

Saffron-Flavored Omelet

serves 1   *calories per serving: 185*   *total fat per serving: 14.6 g*

This omelet is made with an unusual combination of dried cranberries. The saffron provides the color and aroma and the sweetness is supplied by cranberries. The soft omelet provides a pleasant blend of spice and sweet.

Ingredients

2 tablespoons canola oil
3 large eggs, slightly beaten
A large pinch of saffron
½ teaspoon salt
½ jalapeño pepper, seeded, deveined, and minced
1 teaspoon dried cranberries
½ teaspoon garam masala

Method

In an omelet pan, heat some oil.
In a bowl, combine eggs, saffron, salt, and jalapeño pepper. Add this mixture to the pan. Add dried cranberries and garam masala, and fold the omelet. Cook on low heat for 3 minutes. Once the omelet is ready, transfer it to a serving platter and serve hot.

Baked Eggs in Tomato Sauce

serves 4   *calories per serving: 209*   *total fat per serving: 11.8 g*

Baked eggs are commonplace in everyday Indian cooking. Here, eggs are broken into the sauce and then baked in the oven. The result is that the eggs are sitting in the sauce and the sauce becomes silky. The dish is brought to the table directly from the oven.

Ingredients

1 Tablespoon canola oil
2 large onions, peeled and sliced thinly
2 garlic cloves, peeled and sliced thinly
1 teaspoon garam masala
4 tomatoes, cored, seeded, and chopped
½ teaspoon red chili flakes
½ cup water
1 can of coconut milk
6 large eggs
½ cup cilantro leaves, cleaned and chopped coarsely
½ cup parsley leaves, cleaned and chopped finely
Salt to taste

Method

In a large, shallow pan, combine canola oil, onions, garlic, garam masala, and tomatoes. Let it cook for 4–5 minutes. Add chili flakes and water. Then add coconut milk and let it cook for a few minutes. Break the eggs into the mixture and let it cook for a few minutes. Transfer it to the oven for 10 minutes at 300 degrees. Add cilantro and parsley leaves and serve hot.

Eggs with Eggplant and Potatoes

serves 4   calories per serving: 336   total fat per serving: 12.8 g

Eggplant and Potatoes is a good match and both the vegetables have a natural affinity with each other and hold their shape when quickly stir fried. This recipe will work well with Japanese eggplants or small eggplants. This is a good side dish.

Ingredients

6 eggs, extra large
2 Tablespoons canola oil
2 large red onions, peeled and sliced in thin slivers
1 jalapeño pepper, finely chopped
2 cloves garlic, peeled and finely sliced
1 large piece of ginger, finely chopped
8 curry leaves
½ teaspoon mustard seeds
½ teaspoon turmeric powder
½ teaspoon garam masala
½ teaspoon coriander powder
¼ teaspoon cumin powder
3 tomatoes, finely sliced
2 Japanese eggplants, cut into thin rounds
1 large potato, cut into rounds or cubes
2 Tablespoons fresh grated coconut
3 Tablespoons cilantro leaves, chopped finely
Salt to taste

Method

Insert the eggs in a largish saucepan, fill the pan with water, and let it come to a boil. This takes approximately 10 minutes. Remove the eggs and transfer into an ice bath. Keep the eggs in the ice bath for 10 minutes and then peel the shells away. Chop the eggs into medium-sized pieces.

In another pan, heat the oil and add onions, chilies, garlic, ginger, curry leaves, mustard seeds, turmeric, garam masala, coriander, cumin, tomatoes, eggplants, and potatoes. Sauté this vegetable mixture for a few minutes or until the vegetables are cooked. Add fresh grated coconut. Add the cooked eggs and cilantro, and salt to taste.

Quick Egg Curry

serves 4   *calories per serving: 174*   *total fat per serving: 11.2 g*

An egg curry is made with boiled eggs. The egg and the curry will cook together, allowing the eggs to absorb some of the wonderful curry flavor.

Ingredients

6 large eggs
2 Tablespoons canola oil
2 red onions, peeled and finely chopped
2 cloves garlic, peeled and finely chopped
1 large piece of ginger, peeled and finely chopped
4 Tablespoons unsweetened dry coconut flakes
¼ teaspoon turmeric powder
1 teaspoon coriander powder
1 teaspoon peppercorns, crushed in a mortar and pestle
¼ teaspoon cumin powder
2 dry red chilies
2 tomatoes, chopped into small pieces
4 Tablespoons cilantro leaves
Salt to taste

Method

Put eggs in a large saucepan filled with water. Let the water boil, switch off the heat, and let the eggs sit in the water for 10 more minutes. Transfer the eggs into an ice water bath. Remove the eggs. Then peel them and cut them in half. Set the eggs aside. Cut each egg into two halves.

In a small frying pan, combine oil, onions, garlic, ginger, dry coconut flakes, turmeric powder, coriander powder, peppercorns, cumin powder, red chilies, and tomatoes. Fry all this until the coconut becomes a golden honey color.

Grind this mixture into a paste. Keep this aside.

In another medium-sized saucepan, cook the ground mixture for a minute. Add the eggs and ½ cup water, and cook for 10 minutes. Add salt to taste and garnish with cilantro leaves.

Innovative Indian Cuisine

Chicken

Indians love chicken and often prefer it to other birds, like duck and quail, which are expensive. The chicken is usually spiced and marinated before grilling, baking, or even cooking in a curry. The dishes in this book, such as Cinnamon Chicken, Mango Chutney Chicken, and Garbanzo Chicken, are deeply satisfying with rice or bread.

Garbanzo Chicken

serves 4   calories per serving: 403   total fat per serving: 11.8g

Garbanzo beans are often used in Indian cooking and are combined with many different vegetables. Here I have combined the garbanzo beans with chicken to create a chicken dish with a slightly different taste. The garbanzo beans add a surprisingly creamy texture to the chicken.

Ingredients

2 Tablespoon canola oil
4 cardamom pods, skinned and ground to a fine powder
5 cloves, ground into powder
¼ cup dry unsweetened coconut flakes
½ teaspoon poppy seeds
12 peppercorns
¼ teaspoon fennel seeds
1 teaspoon cinnamon powder
1 teaspoon coriander powder
3 dried chilies arbol
1 large onion, peeled and chopped finely
6 skinless, boneless chicken thighs
2 cloves of garlic, peeled and chopped finely
1-inch piece of ginger, peeled and chopped finely
½ teaspoon turmeric powder
1 teaspoon cumin seeds
1 bay leaf, dry or fresh
2 cups of nonfat plain yogurt
1 cup of water

2 cups of boiled garbanzo beans or 2 cups of canned garbanzo beans

1 teaspoon garam masala

Salt to taste

½ cup to 1 cup cilantro leaves

Method

In a small pan, pour 2 Tablespoons oil. Add cardamom powder, clove powder, coconut flakes, poppy seeds, peppercorns, fennel seeds, cinnamon, and coriander, and chilies arbol. Sauté for a few minutes until it turns golden brown. Put this mixture in the mixer and grind it into a paste.

In a large vessel, combine the remaining oil and onions. Sauté the onions until golden brown. Next, add chicken and brown it. Add garlic, ginger, turmeric, cumin seeds, and bay leaf. Add the ground mixture to the pot.

Let it cook for a few minutes and add 2 cups of yogurt mixed with 1 cup of water. Cover and let the chicken cook in this sauce for 25 minutes on low heat. Add water if the sauce is too thick and heavy. A good sauce should not be too thin and watery; nor should it be so thick that it doesn't move quickly.

Add garbanzo beans, garam masala, salt, and cilantro. Let the chicken cook in the sauce, along with the garbanzo beans, for 10 minutes. Serve hot.

Green Chicken

serves 4   *calories per serving: 287*   *total fat per serving: 12.7 g*

Chicken is combined with green herbs to make a green sauce in which the chicken floats. The different herbs, such as cilantro, oregano, basil, and mint, produce a zesty and robust sauce that's flavorful and vibrant in color.

Ingredients

1 Tablespoon garlic paste
1 Tablespoon ginger paste
1 green jalapeño chili, minced with the seeds
1 Tablespoon canola oil
2 medium-sized red onions, peeled and chopped
1 pound of boneless chicken, cut into bite-size pieces
2 heaped Tablespoons of mint chutney
1 Tablespoon oregano leaves
1 cup cilantro leaves, washed and chopped coarsely
1 cup of basil leaves, finely chopped
2 teaspoons almond paste
2 teaspoons coriander powder
½ teaspoon garam masala
1 cup nonfat yogurt
4 Tablespoons water
Salt to taste

Method

Make a paste of garlic, ginger, and green chili with a few teaspoons of water in a mixer or food processor.

Take a medium-sized pot, add oil, and sauté the onions for a few minutes. Then add the chicken and let this cook for a few minutes. Add the ginger, garlic, and chili paste mixture and let it cook for a few minutes.

In a food processor, make another paste of mint chutney, oregano, cilantro, basil, and almond paste. Add this paste to the pot. Now add coriander, garam masala, and salt. Add yogurt and water, stir it together, and let it cook on low heat for 30 minutes.

Cinnamon Chicken

serves 4   *calories per serving: 307*   *total fat per serving: 13.1 g*

Cinnamon is a strong spice, and, if used in large quantities, can be overwhelming. Cinnamon chicken is a wonderful dish and is used with yogurt and cream to produce a silky sauce.

Ingredients

2 Tablespoon canola oil
1 large red onion
2 teaspoons turmeric powder
8 bone-in chicken thighs, skinless
2 red chilies arbol
1 large piece of ginger, peeled and chopped finely
4 large garlic cloves, peeled and chopped finely
2 teaspoons cinnamon powder
1 teaspoon smoked paprika
1 cup water
½ teaspoon sugar
1 cup nonfat yogurt
½ cup chopped cilantro leaves
Salt to taste

Method

In a large vessel, combine oil, half of the garlic cloves, red onion, turmeric powder, and chicken. Let the chicken marinate for at least 30 minutes. Brown the chicken. Remove the chicken pieces and set aside.

In a mixer, grind chilies, ginger, the remaining garlic, cinnamon powder, and water.

Add the onion-turmeric-garlic mixture and the paprika, and additional water to create a sauce. Add the chicken back to the pot and let it cook on medium heat for 10 minutes.

Add yogurt and let the chicken cook for another 30–35 minutes. Add cilantro and salt to the cooked chicken.

Creamy Chicken Kebabs

serves 4   *calories per serving: 435*   *total fat per serving: 16.9 g*

Chicken skewered in cream—kebab style. Chicken breasts are cut into two-inch pieces and marinated in sour cream to give them that slightly tangy flavor. The cashews add richness, and the saffron releases a sweet aroma when the chicken is cooked.

Ingredients

2 teaspoons canola oil
1 cup nonfat sour cream
¼ cup cashews, ground into a paste
½ teaspoon cayenne pepper
½ teaspoon saffron
1 Tablespoon garam masala
Salt and pepper to taste
3 chicken breasts, cubed
2 lemons, juiced

Method

Marinate the chicken in sour cream, cashew paste, cayenne pepper, saffron, and garam masala. Add salt and pepper to taste. Let the chicken marinate in this mixture for at least 4 hours.

Grill the chicken and baste it with the remaining marinade if available. If no marinade remains, baste with a few tablespoons of oil. Garnish with lemon juice. Serve with a salad or bread.

Easy Mango Chutney Chicken

serves 4   *calories per serving: 369*   *total fat per serving: 20.2 g*

This is a very easy dish where two store-bought ingredients are combined to make a marinade. When you bite into the chicken, the flavors mingle, bringing forth surprising sweet and minty flavors.

Ingredients

4 Tablespoons fresh lime juice
4 bone-in chicken breasts
1 Tablespoon olive oil
3 Tablespoons cilantro leaves, chopped finely
3 Tablespoons of store-bought sweet mango chutney
3 Tablespoons of store-bought mint chutney
Salt to taste

Method

Pour 2 Tablespoons lime juice in a large nonreactive bowl. Now add the chicken, olive oil, a little bit of salt, and chopped cilantro, and let it sit in this marinade for 15 minutes.

Add mango chutney and mint chutney to the chicken, and let it sit in the marinade for 4 hours.

Bake the chicken at 450 degrees for 12–15 minutes. Now lower the heat to 350 degrees and bake for 15 more minutes. Broil the chicken for 5 minutes. Take care that the chicken does not dry.

When the chicken is done, remove from the oven, squeeze remaining limejuice over the chicken, and salt and pepper if required. Serve hot.

Asian Corn Fritters

Asparagus with Spinach

Baked Eggs in Tomato Sauce

Basil and Red Pepper Rice

Braised Lamb with Root Vegetables

Chilled Mango Soup

Cinnamon Chicken

Creamy Avocado Salad

Creamy Chicken Kebabs

Fish Crusted in Potato

Fish in Banana Leaves

Lamb in White Sauce

Mango Tart

Pink Raspberry Pudding

Potato Pancakes

Quick Egg Curry

Saffrom Flavored Omlette

Scrambled Egg with Shrimp

Shrimp Fritters with Goat Cheese

Shrimp in Herb Sauce

Shrimp Pilaf

Snappy Pickled Potatoes

Spicy Lentils

Spicy Meatballs

Spicy Pumpkin Soup

Stuffed Red Peppers

Sweet Saffron Pudding

Sweet Stuffed Banana Bread

Tandoori Chicken

Vanilla Vermicelli Pudding

Zesty Lamb Chops

Zucchini Pancakes

Apricot Chicken

serves 4–6   calories per serving: 340   *total fat per serving: 17.1 g*

This is a chicken curry with tomatoes and apricots. Apricots are used to enhance the color and introduce a sweetish taste. This is a simple dish, and the combination of chicken and apricots is exotic.

Ingredients

1 Tablespoon canola oil
1 large onion, minced and chopped finely
1-inch piece of ginger, peeled and diced finely
2 large cloves of garlic
2 cans of diced tomatoes
2 fresh green jalapeños, deseeded and minced
1 cinnamon stick
1 Tablespoon coriander powder
1 teaspoon cumin powder
1 teaspoon garam masala
1 pound of skinless, boneless chicken breasts, cut into 2-inch pieces
8 dried apricots, chopped coarsely
1 cup nonfat yogurt
1 Tablespoon light cream
½ cup cilantro leaves
½ cup parsley leaves
1 cup water
Salt to taste

Method

In a large Dutch oven, combine oil, onions, ginger, garlic, tomatoes, and green chilies, and fry for 8 minutes or so. Add cinnamon stick, coriander, cumin, and garam masala.

Add chicken, apricot pieces, and yogurt. Let it cook for a few minutes. Then add 1 cup water and let it cook for 30 minutes or until the chicken is done. Add cream and cook for 2 minutes. Add cilantro and parsley. Serve hot.

Pomegranate Grilled Chicken

serves 4   *calories per serving: 228*   *total fat per serving: 8.5 g*

Chicken is marinated in pomegranate molasses and grilled. The molasses gives the chicken a sweet and tart flavor. Note that the molasses can burn the chicken if you are not careful. This dish also has a gingery flavor which counterbalances the sweetness that the molasses imparts.

Ingredients

1 Tablespoon ginger, peeled and mashed
3 cloves garlic, peeled and mashed
4 chicken breasts with bone, rinsed and patted dry
1 Tablespoon garam masala
½ teaspoon cayenne pepper
1 Tablespoon olive oil
½ cup pomegranate molasses
Salt and pepper to taste
4 Tablespoons lemon juice

Method

Apply ginger and garlic paste to the chicken, and sprinkle garam masala and cayenne pepper on top. Add olive oil, pomegranate molasses, and salt and pepper to taste. Marinate for 4 hours. Next, bake the chicken for 45 minutes at 350 degrees. Broil the chicken for 5 minutes or until slightly charred. Remove the chicken from the oven and let cool for 5 minutes. Add lemon juice, and sprinkle it with cayenne pepper if needed.

Garlic Chicken

serves 4–6   calories per serving: 391   *total fat per serving: 26.6 g*

Lots of garlic is used in Indian cooking. A combination of ginger and garlic with onions is often used to create a delicious sauce. However, in this dish, only garlic is used, to produce a delicious garlicky chicken. This is a baked dish and does not require much time to prepare.

Ingredients

1 whole chicken, cut up into serving-size pieces
2 whole heads of garlic, peeled into cloves and cut into halves
2 cups chicken stock
2 lemons, cut and juiced
1 teaspoon cumin powder
1 Tablespoon coriander powder
½ teaspoon cayenne pepper
2 bay leaves
1 Tablespoon canola oil
1 cup cilantro leaves
1 cup coconut milk
1 teaspoon garam masala
Salt to taste

Method

In a large baking dish, combine chicken, garlic, chicken stock, lemon juice, cumin, coriander, cayenne pepper, bay leaves, and canola oil.

Bake the dish at 300 degrees in a preheated oven for 1 hour.

Remove the dish from the oven and add cilantro leaves, coconut milk, and garam masala, and cook for 10 minutes so that the coconut milk gets warm.

Chicken with Mushrooms

serves 4–6   calories per serving: 301   total fat per serving: 12.8 g

Mushrooms have an earthy quality and a musky flavor.
Chicken when combined with mushrooms gives the curry
certain meatiness and depth. Note that shiitake mushrooms
are used here but you can choose your favorite type of
mushrooms to make this dish.

Ingredients

1 Tablespoon canola oil
6 skinless, bone-in chicken thighs
1 cinnamon stick
4 cloves
1 large black cardamom pod whole
6 peppercorns
2–4 red chilies
1 bay leaf
1 teaspoon turmeric powder
½ teaspoon cumin powder
1 teaspoon coriander powder
2 cans of canned tomatoes
2 pounds of shiitake mushrooms
1 cup nonfat yogurt
1 cup cilantro leaves, chopped finely
Salt to taste

Method

Pour the oil in a large pot and brown the chicken. Add the cinnamon, cloves, cardamom, peppercorns, red chilies, bay leaf, turmeric, cumin, coriander, and tomatoes. Add the mushrooms and let cook in the gravy for 15 minutes. Add a little water if it looks too dry.

Now add 1 Tablespoon of yogurt and stir well. Add the rest of the yogurt a tablespoon at a time to make sure that the yogurt is smooth and doesn't curdle.

Add cilantro leaves and salt to taste, and serve hot.

Stuffed Chicken Breasts

serves 6   calories per serving: 417   total fat per serving: 26.0 g

In this recipe, chicken is marinated with mint and cilantro and baked. The chicken is marinated for 6 hours and stuffed with ground lamb, pine nuts, and mint leaves. Stuffed chicken is not a common dish, and is only cooked during festive occasions.

Ingredients for Marinade

1 Tablespoon canola oil
½ teaspoon cayenne pepper
1 teaspoon turmeric powder
3 large garlic cloves, minced finely
3 teaspoons ginger, minced finely
4 Tablespoons lemon juice
1 Tablespoons garam masala
Salt to taste
6 chicken breasts, rinsed and patted dry

Ingredients for Stuffing

1 Tablespoon canola oil
2 large red onions, minced finely
3 large garlic cloves
1 teaspoon ginger paste
1 Tablespoon coriander powder
1 teaspoon cumin powder
¾ pound ground lamb
2 large eggs, lightly beaten
3 teaspoons lemon zest

1 cup cilantro leaves, washed and chopped coarsely
1 cup mint leaves, washed and chopped coarsely
1 cup pine nuts, roasted until golden brown and chopped
4 teaspoons lemon juice
Salt to taste

Method

In a large, shallow vessel, pour all the ingredients for the marinade and place the chicken in the marinade. Let the chicken marinate for at least 6 hours.

Next, in a medium-sized sauté pan, add 1 Tablespoon canola oil. Add onions, garlic, ginger, coriander, cumin, and ground lamb. Let this cook for 20–25 minutes. Now add eggs, lemon zest, cilantro, mint, pine nuts, and lemon juice, and cook for 5 minutes. Let this mixture cool down before stuffing the chicken.

Remove the marinated chicken breasts and make a pocket. Stuff the chicken with the lamb mixture, and place it on a baking dish. Fill all the chicken breasts this way, and bake for 35–40 minutes at 350 degrees.

Broil the chicken for 3–4 minutes to get the charred marks, if desired.

Chicken with Carrot Sauce

serves 4   calories per serving: 465   total fat per serving: 15.5 g

In this recipe, chicken is teamed with carrots to create a sweet and flavorful sauce. The chilies impart spiciness, and the nonfat yogurt and cream create a tangy sauce. Carrots are not often used with chicken in Indian cuisine, but this vegetable is highly nutritious and creates a sweetish sauce which is pleasing to the palate.

Ingredients

2 Tablespoons canola oil
2 large red onions, peeled and chopped finely
2 Tablespoons ginger, peeled and finely chopped
Salt and pepper to taste
½ teaspoon cayenne pepper
1 Tablespoon coriander powder
1 teaspoon cumin powder
2 teaspoons garam masala
1 cup carrot juice
2 green chilies, like jalapeños, stemmed, seeded, and minced
2 cups nonfat yogurt
2 pounds boneless chicken breasts, cut into bite-size pieces
1 Tablespoon light cream
4 Tablespoons cilantro leaves, chopped coarsely for garnish

Method

Put the oil in a flameproof dish over medium-high heat. Add the oil, onions, and one tablespoon ginger, along with salt and pepper to taste, and cook, stirring occasionally, until the onions start turning golden brown.

Add the cayenne pepper, coriander, and cumin. Let it cook 2 minutes with the onion mixture.

In another saucepan, brown the chicken with 1 Tablespoon oil. Transfer the chicken onto a platter, sprinkle it with 1 teaspoon garam masala, and set aside.

Grind the carrot juice, remaining ginger, green chilies and nonfat yogurt in the blender until the sauce becomes smooth and velvety in consistency. (You can make the sauce in advance.)

Now add the chicken to the onion mixture, and then add the carrot-ginger sauce. Cook the chicken for 30 minutes in the sauce. Add a teaspoon of garam masala. Add light cream, and garnish with cilantro leaves. Serve this on a bed of steamed rice.

Basil Cilantro Chicken

serves 4   calories per serving: 350   total fat per serving: 15.2 g

Basil and cilantro with honey make a fantastic combination where savory and sweet mix together to give a wonderful flavoring to the chicken. Sherry vinegar gives tartness to the recipe. Marinate for a minimum of 4 hours to allow the flavors to blend well.

Ingredients

1 Tablespoon of olive oil
4 chicken breasts
¼ cup of sherry vinegar
2 Tablespoons soy sauce
¼ cup honey
5 Tablespoons basil leaves, chopped finely
3 Tablespoons cilantro leaves, chopped finely
2 teaspoons ginger
½ teaspoon red chili flakes
2 teaspoons garlic
1 teaspoon garam masala
Salt to taste

Method

Marinate the chicken with olive oil, sherry vinegar, soy sauce, honey, basil leaves, cilantro leaves, ginger, red chili flakes, and garlic. Keep it in the refrigerator for 4 hours.
Bake the chicken in the oven at 450 degrees for 15 minutes. Reduce the heat to 350 degrees and let it cook for 30 minutes

more. Finally, broil the chicken for 5 minutes and sprinkle it with garam masala. Serve hot.

Chicken Curry with a Twist

serves 4   *calories per serving: 317*   *total fat per serving: 17.5 g*

There are many varieties of chicken curry, and this one has lemongrass which makes for a slightly different twist. Lemongrass also adds a subtle lemony taste to the curry.

Ingredients

1 Tablespoon canola oil
4 bone-in chicken thighs, with skin
2 medium-sized red onions, chopped finely
3 garlic cloves, chopped finely
2 ginger slices, chopped finely
1 teaspoon turmeric powder
2 stalks of lemongrass, kept whole
1 Tablespoon Madras curry powder
2 cups of chicken broth
Salt and pepper to taste
½ cup cilantro leaves

Method

Pour the oil into a large vessel and let it heat up for a few minutes. Add the chicken and fry it until it is cooked through. Add red onions, garlic, ginger, turmeric, lemongrass, and Madras curry powder. Let the chicken cook in this mixture for 3 minutes.

Add chicken broth, salt, and pepper.

Cover the saucepan and let it simmer for 30–45 minutes.

Garnish it with cilantro leaves.

Grilled Chicken with Rose Petals

serves 4   *calories per serving: 343*   *total fat per serving: 17.4 g*

In this unique dish, the chicken is marinated with rose petals, thyme leaves, spices, and lemon juice. The lemon and rose impart a perfume to the chicken during the grilling process.

Ingredients

1 teaspoon dried thyme leaves
1 teaspoon chili powder
1 cup cilantro leaves, washed and chopped coarsely
2 Tablespoons olive oil
4 Tablespoons lemon juice
Salt and pepper to taste
½ cup rose petals (edible)
4 chicken breasts
2 lemons, cut into wedges for garnish

Method

In a small bowl, combine the thyme, chili powder, cilantro, olive oil, lemon juice, salt, pepper, and rose petals.
Add the chicken and coat it thoroughly with the marinade. Let it marinate for 6 hours.
Grill the chicken until it is done, and serve it with lemon wedges.

Tandoori Chicken

serves 4   calories per serving: 386   total fat per serving: 18.6 g

Tandoori chicken is a very popular Indian dish. Here, chickpea flour is added to give some thickness to the marinade, and mint and cilantro leaves are added to increase the flavor of the marinade. Take care that the mint does not overwhelm the tandoori chicken taste.

Ingredients

4 pieces of skinless chicken, thighs or breasts
4 green chilies, deseeded and chopped finely
1 large piece of ginger, peeled and chopped finely
6 garlic cloves, peeled and chopped finely
1 Tablespoon garam masala
2 teaspoons curry powder
2 cups nonfat yogurt, drained well
2 teaspoons chickpea flour
1 cup cilantro leaves, coarsely chopped
½ cup mint leaves, coarsely chopped
Salt and pepper to taste
4 Tablespoons lemon juice
2 lemons, cut into wedges

Method

Place the chicken in a large nonmetallic bowl and poke it with a kitchen knife.

In a mixer, combine green chilies, ginger, garlic, garam masala, curry powder, yogurt, chickpea flour, cilantro, mint, salt, pepper, and lemon juice. Grind this into a smooth paste. Pour this marinade onto the chicken and let it marinate in the fridge for 24 hours.

Preheat the oven to 400 degrees and let the chicken cook for 15 minutes. Reduce the temperature to 350 degrees and let it cook for 25 more minutes. Finally, run the chicken under the broiler for 3 minutes to give it that smoky flavor. Serve with lemon wedges.

Lamb

In India, the common meat is goat meat, which has more bones and less meat than lamb. It has less fat and is healthier. Meat is generally browned to give it a caramelized flavor. Lamb can be cooked in a stew or grilled. For stewing, neck and shank are the best pieces and require a longer cooking time. The meat is usually marinated with vinegar or yogurt for long periods of time to break the fibers and tenderize the meat, and also to allow the flavors to blend with each other.

Spicy Meatballs

serves 4   *calories per serving: 361*   *total fat per serving: 12.3g*

Meatballs are teamed up with spinach and eggs to make this savory dish. This makes a nice appetizer when molded into tiny balls, or a main dish when made into big meatballs. The egg and spinach add a different dimension in texture and taste.

Ingredients

1 pound ground lamb with some fat for flavor
½ bag of baby spinach leaves, cut into chiffonade (thin strips)
1 or 2 green chilies, such as jalapeños, deseeded and deveined
1 teaspoon cinnamon powder
1 teaspoon garlic paste or garlic chopped finely
1 teaspoon ginger paste or ginger chopped finely
1 teaspoon garam masala
2 large eggs, boiled, peeled and chopped into small cubes
1 cup cilantro leaves, washed and coarsely chopped
1 teaspoon salt
1½ cups store-bought bread crumbs, plain
¼ cup canola oil
4 Tablespoons lemon juice

Method

In a large bowl, combine ground lamb, spinach, green chilies, cinnamon, garlic, ginger, garam masala, boiled egg cubes, and cilantro leaves. Add salt and breadcrumbs.
Mix all the ingredients into a bowl and make round balls about 1½-inches in diameter. Flatten the balls by pressing gently and

place them on a plate. Refrigerate for 2 hours or so.

Heat a shallow pan with oil and when the oil is hot lower the meatballs in the pan gently, a few at time. Do not move them in the oil or turn them quickly. When the balls start to look firm in the oil, flip them and fry until golden brown.

Transfer the hot meatballs onto a platter lined with paper towels. Sprinkle lemon juice on top of the meatballs. Add salt if necessary, and serve.

Chili Lamb Leg

serves 6   *calories per serving: 654*   *total fat per serving: 26.8 g*

Leg of lamb roasted in the oven creates an aroma in the whole house. The lamb needs to be cooked at least 2 ½ hours and should be slightly pink. The spices give the pungent taste and aroma to this recipe, and the addition of honey perfumes the lamb with sweetness.

Ingredients

1 boneless leg of lamb
6 lemons, sliced and juiced
2 Tablespoons olive oil
1 teaspoon cumin powder
2 teaspoons coriander powder
1 teaspoon chili powder
1 teaspoon salt
6 garlic cloves, sliced thinly and made into a paste
10–12 thyme sprigs, leaves removed and chopped finely
¼ cup orange blossom honey
1 teaspoon garam masala

Method

Butterfly the leg of lamb and add half of the lemon juice. Set aside the other half of the lemon juice so that this can be used at the end when the lamb is cooked. Rub olive oil, cumin, coriander, chili powder, salt, garlic paste, and thyme leaves on the lamb, inside and outside.

Let the lamb sit in this mixture for 6–8 hours or so. Place the lamb on a roasting rack and place 1½ cups of water in the bottom of the roasting pan. Take care that the water does not touch the lamb. Roast the lamb at 350 degrees for 1½ hours. Add orange blossom honey and garam masala and roast the lamb at 325 degrees for 40–45 minutes.

Remove the lamb from the oven and place it on a cutting board. Let it cool for 15 minutes so that the juices are absorbed. Slice into paper-thin pieces and serve.

Honeyed Lamb Chops with Cumin

serves 4   calories per serving: 393   total fat per serving: 13.5 g

Lamb chops are a favorite and are paired with honey and cumin to make them savory. The addition of kasuri methi gives a mildly bitter taste that complements the sweetness of the honey very well.

Ingredients

8–10 lamb rib chops
1 teaspoon olive oil
3 cloves of garlic, peeled and chopped finely
1 teaspoon cumin powder
½ teaspoon clove powder
1 teaspoon chili powder
1 teaspoon kasuri methi
¼ cup clover honey
1 teaspoon salt
1 teaspoon pepper

Method

Marinate the lamb chops with olive oil, garlic, cumin, clove, chili powder, kasuri methi, honey, salt, and freshly ground pepper. Marinate in this mixture for 4 hours.
Grill the chops and serve hot.

Zesty Lamb Chops

serves 4–6   calories per serving: 498   *total fat per serving: 23.0 g*

Lamb chops with sherry vinegar and Indian spices give a good combination of flavors. This particular lamb chop recipe has a lot of flavor, with the vinegar and the spices mixed along with a slightly bitter flavor.

Ingredients

2 racks of lamb
6 Tablespoons sherry vinegar
Salt to taste
1 teaspoon smoked paprika
1 teaspoon cayenne pepper
8 garlic cloves, peeled and minced finely
1 Tablespoon garam masala, and extra for sprinkling at the end
Juice of 1 lemon, and extra for sprinkling at the end
4 Tablespoons chickpea flour
1 Tablespoon kasuri methi
2 Tablespoons olive oil

Method

Wash the lamb rack and rub sherry vinegar onto it. Sprinkle it with salt, paprika, and cayenne powder.

In a mixer, combine garlic, garam masala, lemon juice, chickpea flour, salt, and kasuri methi with some oil. Grind this mixture into a paste.

Rub this mixture over the lamb chops and let them marinate for 6 hours or more.

Grill the lamb chops at 450 degrees for 8 minutes or so. Then reduce the temp to 325 degrees and cook for 12–15 minutes or until the rack of lamb is done.

Sprinkle the lamb chops with garam masala and lemon juice before serving.

Lamb with White Sauce

serves 6   *calories per serving: 500*   *total fat per serving: 21.7 g*

This is a lamb curry with the strong spices, but instead of using chicken broth or water, we use milk as the liquid medium. The milk gives a warm, mellow flavor to the lamb, and spices give pungency to the curry.

Ingredients

2 pounds of lamb, cut in big cubes
1 Tablespoon canola oil
2 fresh bay leaves
2 green chilies, deseeded and minced finely
Salt to taste
½ teaspoon sugar
1 cup cilantro leaves as a garnish
1 cup 1% milk

Ingredients for Marinade

8 cloves of garlic, sliced thinly
4 inches ginger, peeled and minced
1 Tablespoon cardamom powder
½ teaspoon nutmeg
1 teaspoon mace
3 cloves
2 cups nonfat yogurt

Method

Grind all the marinade ingredients and marinate the lamb for 6–8 hours.

In a large vessel, heat the oil and brown the lamb. Add bay leaves, chilies, salt, and sugar.

Add the remaining marinade and the milk; if the liquid is too thick, add a ½ cup water to thin it out. Let the lamb cook in this for 1½ to 2 hours in the oven at 350 degrees. Serve hot.

Spicy Lamb Stew

serves 4   calories per serving: 499   total fat per serving: 23.6 g

This spicy stew requires a long simmering process to soften the fibers so that the meat becomes very tender and falls away from the bone. Stews can be made ahead, and the flavors generally improve if made a day ahead.

Ingredients for Marinade

1 large piece ginger, peeled and chopped finely
4 cloves garlic, peeled and chopped finely
½ cup cilantro leaves, chopped finely
1 green chili, deseeded and chopped finely
½ teaspoon turmeric powder
1 cup nonfat yogurt
Salt to taste

Ingredients for Stew

2 pounds lamb meat, preferably leg or shoulder
2 Tablespoons canola oil
2 red onions, peeled and chopped finely
5 cloves
1 stick cinnamon
4 cardamom pods, seeds removed
½ teaspoon poppy seeds
½ teaspoon peppercorns
1 teaspoon fennel seeds
2 teaspoons coriander seeds
1 teaspoon cumin seeds

5 red chilies arbol, broken into pieces
½ teaspoon nutmeg
1 cup grated unsweetened coconut
2 cups water
1 cup cilantro leaves
Salt to taste

Method

Grind ginger, garlic, cilantro, green chilies, turmeric, yogurt, and salt.

Rub this mixture on the meat and keep it in the refrigerator.

In a mixer, combine oil, red onions, cloves, cinnamon stick, cardamom seeds, poppy seeds, peppercorns, fennel seeds, coriander seeds, cumin seeds, chilies, nutmeg, and coconut.

Grind this into a paste; if the mixture is thick, add water.

Scoop the paste into a saucepan and fry until it starts turning golden brown. Add the lamb and let the paste and lamb cook for a few minutes so that the flavors are well blended.

Add 2 cups of water and let it cook on a low heat for 1 hour and 15 minutes or until the meat is cooked and is almost falling off the bone.

Add cilantro leaves and serve.

Braised Lamb with Root Vegetables

serves 4   calories per serving: 604   total fat per serving: 22.4 g

In this recipe, the meat is cooked with root vegetables, and it can also be made with different vegetables of your liking. The vegetables and the lamb are cooked together until the vegetables and lamb are almost falling apart.

Ingredients

1 Tablespoon canola oil
3 large red onions, peeled and chopped finely
5 cloves garlic, peeled and sliced finely
1 teaspoon peppercorns, crushed
2 pounds lamb, meat from leg or shoulder
4 large carrots, peeled and cut into big pieces
2 parsnips cut into big pieces
2 turnips, peeled and cut into big pieces
2 chilies arbol, cut into small pieces
2 teaspoons coriander powder
1 teaspoon cumin powder
¼ teaspoon nutmeg
¼ teaspoon mace
1 teaspoon garam masala
1 can of nonfat yogurt
4 Tablespoons lemon juice
1 teaspoon lemon zest
Salt to taste
2 cups water

Method

In a saucepan, combine oil, onions, garlic, crushed peppercorns, and lamb. Brown the lamb well.

Add carrots, parsnips, and turnips and cook this for a few minutes. Let these flavors blend with the meat. Add chilies, coriander, cumin, nutmeg, mace, garam masala and 2 cups water. Let this simmer for an hour. Take care that the liquid does not evaporate. Add more water if necessary.

Now slowly add 1 can of yogurt, one or two spoons at a time. Let this cook for 30 minutes or so. Add lemon juice, lemon zest, and salt at the end. Serve hot.

Spicy Lamb Curry

serves 4   *calories per serving: 481*   *total fat per serving: 20.3 g*

This is a simple lamb curry made with a few ingredients, including spices that are left intact. These whole spices impart a delicious aroma to the curry. The coconut milk makes this curry mild and acts as a nice buffer to the pungent whole spices.

Ingredients

1 Tablespoon canola oil
2 pounds lamb, cut into stewing pieces
2 large red onions, peeled and chopped finely
1 stick cinnamon
1 bay leaf
4 cloves, crushed into powder
1 teaspoon paprika
4 cloves of garlic, peeled and chopped finely
1 large piece of ginger, peeled and finely chopped
¼ teaspoon asafetida
1 green chili, deseeded and chopped finely
1½ cups of water
1 can of coconut milk
2 Tablespoons cilantro leaves, chopped finely
Salt to taste

Method

In a saucepan, combine oil, lamb, onions, cinnamon, bay leaf, cloves, paprika, garlic, ginger, asafetida, and green chili. Let this cook in its juices. Add 1½ cups water and let it simmer on low heat. Cover and let this cook for 60 to 70 minutes. Add coconut milk and let it cook for 15 minutes. Add cilantro leaves, salt to taste, and serve hot.

Fish and Shellfish

In India, fish is a delicacy and is consumed with much relish along the coastal areas. When buying fresh fish, the eyes must be bright, the gills red, and the skin should look and smell fresh. Fish cannot be overcooked, as this may lead to disintegration of the fish or produce a tough and leathery texture. Fish is usually marinated with spices and herbs to remove any fishy smell. It can be stewed, pan-fried, baked, or grilled. Pan-fried Fish with Mint-Ginger Sauce or Cashew-Crusted Salmon are perfect for a delightful meal.

Fish in Paper

serves 4   calories per serving: 305   total fat per serving: 18.7g

Fish is generally fried or made into stews. Here it is wrapped in a rice paper sheet and lightly fried, then served with a yellow curry sauce. Salmon is used here but any firm-fleshed fish will work. The flavor of the marinade is the first layer of flavor on the fish. The yellow curry adds another layer, so the fish has multiple layers of flavor all mingled together.

Ingredients

4 fish fillets, salmon, cut into big chunks
4 rice paper sheets
2 Tablespoons canola oil

Ingredients for Marinade

2 Tablespoons of curry powder
1 teaspoon tamarind paste
2 teaspoons garlic, peeled and minced
1 teaspoon ginger, peeled and minced
Salt and pepper to taste
1 teaspoon paprika
1 cup cilantro leaves, chopped and cut coarsely

Method

Marinate the fish in curry powder, tamarind paste, garlic, ginger, salt, pepper, paprika, and cilantro. Let the fish marinate for about 3–4 hours.

Take fish chunks out of the marinade and wrap each piece in a sheet of rice paper. Encase the fish completely in the rice paper and make individual fish packets. Set the packets on a large platter.

Pour canola oil in a large frying pan. When the oil is hot, insert the fish packets slowly into the hot oil and let it cook on one side for a few minutes; then turn them and let them fry on the other side.

Remove the packets from the oil and place them on a clean paper towel to drain the excess oil. Serve these bundles with Yellow Curry Sauce.

Yellow Curry Sauce

Ingredients

1 teaspoon canola oil
1 stalk lemongrass, cut into pieces
1 large piece of ginger, peeled and cut into pieces
1 green jalapeño chili, deseeded and minced finely
½ teaspoon mustard seeds
8 curry leaves
1 Tablespoon yellow curry paste
1 teaspoon fish sauce
½ teaspoon brown sugar
I Tablespoon lime juice
1 can of coconut milk
A few tablespoons of cilantro leaves
Salt and pepper to taste

Method

In a small vessel, pour canola oil. When the oil starts heating, add lemongrass, ginger, jalapeño pepper, mustard seeds, and curry leaves. Let this blend in the oil for a few minutes.

Add yellow curry paste, fish sauce, brown sugar, lime juice, and coconut milk. Let this simmer for about 4 minutes or until bubbling. Add salt (very little is needed since fish sauce is salty) and pepper to taste. Garnish the sauce with a few tablespoons of cilantro leaves and serve it with the fish.

Fish with Mint-Ginger Sauce

serves 4   *calories per serving: 359*   *total fat per serving: 22.4 g*

Pan-fried fish recipes are common in Indian cuisine, and any firm-flesh fish will do. Here, it is served with mint and ginger sauce. The mint gives it a sharp, refreshing flavor. The spicy lemony sauce goes well with the fried fish and can be served on the side.

Ingredients

4 fish fillets, like catfish or grouper
1 cup Cream of Wheat
2 Tablespoons canola oil

Ingredients for Mint-Ginger Sauce

1 Tablespoon canola oil
3 Tablespoons ginger, peeled, chopped, and minced
1 teaspoon red pepper flakes
1 teaspoon cumin powder
½ teaspoon coriander powder
½ teaspoon cayenne pepper
1 Tablespoon mint leaves, washed and minced finely
2 cups vegetable stock or fish stock
Cilantro and basil leaves
3 lemons, sliced and juiced
Salt and pepper to taste

Method

Dust the fish with Cream of Wheat and salt. Pan-fry the fish for 2 minutes on each side.

For the sauce, combine oil, ginger, red pepper flakes, cumin, coriander, and cayenne pepper in a medium-sized pot. Let this cook for a few minutes, add mint leaves and stock, and let the stock cook for a few minutes until it thickens slightly.

Pour this sauce on the fish. Garnish with cilantro, basil leaves, and lemon juice. Add salt and pepper to taste.

Fish in Banana Leaves

serves 4   calories per serving: 396   total fat per serving: 25.9 g

First the fish is applied with a mixture of various herbs and spices, and then placed in a banana-leaf wrap and baked slowly. The wrapping of the fish creates a steam that will seal the flavors inside the banana-leaf packet, creating a succulent and juicy fish.

Ingredients

1 Tablespoon olive oil
8 curry leaves, sautéed in a little oil
½ cup unsweetened coconut flakes
1 bunch cilantro leaves
½ cup mint leaves
4 large garlic cloves
1 large piece of ginger
¼ teaspoon asafetida
1 cup nonfat yogurt
3 green chilies, deseeded and chopped coarsely
4 boneless fish fillets
4 large squares of banana leaves
Salt and pepper to taste

Method

In a mixer, grind all the ingredients except the fish, banana leaves, salt, and pepper. Make a smooth paste. Keep aside.
Preheat the oven to 350 degrees.
Cut the banana leaves into 4 squares and place the fish on top,

along with little oil. Sprinkle with salt and pepper.
Place a dollop of the cilantro-coconut mixture on top. Add
more if needed. Close the packet and tie it with a string.
Place the packets on the tray and let them cook in the oven at
350 degrees for 20 minutes. Remove them from the oven and
cut open the string. Open the packet and serve hot.

Spicy Fish Stew

serves 4–6   calories per serving: 325   total fat per serving: 17.7 g

Fish stews are wonderful and are a major part of Indian cuisine. This fish stew is spicy with underlying sweet tones. The tomatoes provide a sweetish flavor, whereas the spices, chilies, and vinegar provide a sharp, tangy taste.

Ingredients

1 Tablespoon canola oil
2 teaspoons garlic, peeled and minced finely
1 Tablespoon ginger, peeled and minced
1 jalapeño chili, deseeded and finely minced
1 large onion, peeled and cut into thin slivers
1 teaspoon cumin powder
½ teaspoon coriander powder
2 cans chopped tomatoes
1 red pepper, chopped finely
1 pound fish fillets
2 teaspoons rice vinegar
1 cup cilantro leaves, chopped and minced finely
Salt and pepper to taste

Method

In a Dutch oven, heat oil over medium heat. When the oil gets hot, add garlic, ginger, jalapeño, onions, cumin, and coriander. Let this cook for 5 minutes. Add tomatoes and red pepper. Add the fish fillets and rice vinegar. Add salt and pepper. Let it cook for 15 minutes on low heat. Sprinkle cilantro leaves on top, and serve hot.

Cilantro Snapper

serves 4   *calories per serving: 282*   *total fat per serving: 18.2 g*

Stuffed fish is a festive dish, and the whole fish is presented at the table. You can stuff the fish with different kinds of stuffing. In this recipe, I have used lemons and oranges with cilantro and mint leaves. The use of spices helps remove the fishy smell and adds flavor to the fish.

Ingredients

2 Tablespoons olive oil

3 medium-sized whole red snapper

Salt to taste

¾ teaspoon cayenne powder

1 teaspoon cumin powder

2 teaspoons turmeric powder

1 bunch cilantro leaves, washed and coarsely chopped

1 bunch mint leaves, washed and coarsely chopped

4 lemons, cut into slices and seeded

2 oranges, cut into thick slices

4 garlic cloves, thinly sliced

1 large piece of ginger, peeled and thinly sliced

2 green chilies, deseeded and minced

1 teaspoon chaat masala

Method

Rinse the fish and make horizontal slits in it. Add salt, cayenne powder, cumin, and turmeric to the fish. Let the fish sit with the rub in the refrigerator for 4 hours.

Stuff the fish with cilantro leaves, mint leaves, lemon slices, orange slices, garlic slices, ginger slices, green chilies, and chaat masala. Sprinkle the fish with olive oil.

Grill the fish until cooked or bake the fish at 350 degrees for 25 minutes. If you bake the fish, put it under the broiler for 3 minutes to get that charred flavor.

Shrimp Curry with Orange Zest

serves 4–6   calories per serving: 426   *total fat per serving: 30.3 g*

There are many recipes for shrimp curries, which can be savored with rice as well as bread. Shrimp curry is combined with orange zest and orange juice to give it a slightly different twist. The coconut milk gives it a creamy texture while the red chilies give it a spicy flavor.

Ingredients

1 pound of shrimp, medium-sized, cleaned and deveined
1 teaspoon orange zest
2 teaspoons curry powder (1 teaspoon to marinate and 1 teaspoon for curry)
Salt and pepper to taste
1 Tablespoon olive oil
1 large red onion, finely chopped
1 teaspoon garlic made into a pulp
1 teaspoon ginger made into a pulp
½ teaspoon turmeric powder
8 curry leaves
1 teaspoon mustard seeds
3 dried red chilies
1 teaspoon fenugreek seeds
½ bunch scallions, cleaned and chopped finely
1 Tablespoon orange juice without pulp
1 can light organic coconut milk
1 teaspoon fresh thyme leaves
1 cup cilantro leaves, cleaned and chopped coarsely

Method

Marinate the shrimp in orange zest and 1 teaspoon of curry powder. Also add salt and pepper to the shrimp. Let the shrimp marinate in this mixture for 1 hour or so.

In a medium-sized saucepan, pour the oil and let it sizzle; then add onions, garlic, ginger, turmeric, curry leaves, mustard seeds, chili peppers, fenugreek seeds, and scallions. Cook all this until the onions turn golden brown and an aroma develops.

Add shrimp to this mixture. Let them cook for about 4 minutes or until they turn pink. Add orange juice and coconut milk and let this cook with the mixture on a low simmer for 8 minutes. Garnish it with thyme and cilantro leaves, and serve it with jasmine rice.

Shrimp and Scallop Curry

serves 4   *calories per serving: 469*   *total fat per serving: 17.8 g*

The main thing with this recipe is that two different types of shellfish are combined. The fish dish is a curry with sweet, sour, and spicy overtones. The different flavors of lime and orange juice give the acidity, and the chilies provide spiciness.

Ingredients

1 Tablespoon olive oil
1 medium-sized red onion, minced finely
2 cloves of garlic, peeled and chopped
1 large piece of ginger, peeled and chopped into thin strips
1 stalk lemongrass, chopped into big pieces
1 jalapeño pepper, chopped finely
½ pound of medium-sized shrimp, peeled and deveined
½ pound of medium-sized scallops
1 can of unsweetened coconut milk
2 Tablespoons lime juice
2 Tablespoons orange juice
1 cup cilantro leaves, washed and chopped coarsely
Salt and pepper to taste

Method

Pour olive oil in a wok. When the oil sizzles, add onions, garlic, ginger, lemongrass, and jalapeño pepper, and let it cook until the onions become golden brown.

Add shrimp and scallops and cook for a few minutes. See that the shrimp and scallops are of the same size so that they cook at an even pace. Add coconut milk. Let this simmer for 5 minutes so that the shrimp do not overcook and become tough.

Add lime juice, orange juice, and cilantro at the end. Serve hot.

Scallops with Cream

serves 4   calories per serving: 199   total fat per serving: 11.0 g

Scallops are easy to cook. Sautéed or grilled, they cook quickly and are usually put in a curry or served with a sauce, as here. The cilantro cream provides a greenish color and a creamy texture.

Ingredients

1 Tablespoon canola oil
1 pound scallops, washed and cleaned
4 Tablespoons lime juice
Salt and pepper to taste
½ teaspoon cumin powder
¼ teaspoon cayenne pepper
½ teaspoon salt
1 cup cilantro leaves, washed and chopped

Ingredients for Cilantro Cream

½ cup nonfat sour cream
1 cup nonfat yogurt
½ cup chopped cilantro leaves
Salt and pepper to taste

Method

Marinate the scallops in lime juice, half a teaspoon salt, cumin, cayenne pepper, and cilantro. Let it sit for 1 hour or so.
Mix the ingredients of the cilantro cream in a medium bowl and stir well. Pan-fry the scallops and serve with cilantro cream.

Cashew-Crusted Salmon

serves 4   *calories per serving: 347*   *total fat per serving: 24.1 g*

This is an easy dish to make that can impress guests. Salmon is first dipped in egg and cashew powder and then fried with panko breadcrumbs. I have used salmon here, but other kinds of fish, such as snapper, will work fine.

Ingredients

2 Tablespoons canola oil
4 salmon pieces
2 large eggs, beaten slightly
1 cup of ground cashew nuts
2 teaspoons cilantro leaves or 2 teaspoons thyme leaves
½ cup unsweetened coconut flakes
1 cup panko breadcrumbs
1 teaspoon turmeric powder
1 teaspoon garam masala
½ teaspoon red pepper flakes
Salt to taste

Method

Dip the salmon in egg, drain the excess, and dip this in cashew powder, finely chopped cilantro or thyme leaves, coconut flakes, turmeric powder, garam masala, and red pepper flakes. Now layer the salmon pieces with panko breadcrumbs.

In a large, shallow pan, pour canola oil and slowly insert the salmon. Let it cook on one side and then turn it and fry on the other side. Serve hot.

Shrimp with Herb Sauce

serves 4–6   calories per serving: 306   *total fat per serving: 10.5 g*

This is a dish in which shrimp is paired with a medley of herbs such as cilantro, mint, and basil to produce a light sauce. The addition of some cream gives depth and richness to the sauce.

Ingredients

2 cloves garlic, peeled and chopped finely
2 green jalapeño peppers, deseeded and finely chopped
½ teaspoon garam masala
½ cup mint leaves, washed and chopped coarsely
1 cup cilantro leaves, washed and chopped coarsely
¾ cup basil leaves, washed and chopped coarsely
1 Tablespoon light cream
1 Tablespoon olive oil
2 pounds of shrimp, peeled, cleaned, and deveined
Salt and pepper to taste

Method

In a food processor or mixer, combine garlic, jalapeño, garam masala, mint leaves, cilantro, and basil. Add cream, and grind this mixture into a smooth paste.

In a medium-sized pan, pour olive oil and let it cook for a minute or so. Add shrimp, and let the shrimp cook in the olive oil. Now add the green sauce and let the shrimp and the sauce cook together for 5–8 minutes. Add salt and pepper to taste, and serve hot with rice.

Fish or Shrimp in Potato

serves 4   calories per serving: 395   total fat per serving: 18.5 g

Any fish or shrimp can be crusted with different vegetables and pan-fried. Potato, with its high starch content, makes a crusty exterior with the fish remaining moist inside. Other vegetables can be used, such as zucchini, sweet potato, and parsnips.

Ingredients

1 pound of large shrimp, cleaned and deveined
1 large piece of ginger, peeled and minced finely
3 cloves of garlic, peeled and minced finely
1 cup of cilantro leaves, washed and chopped finely
1 jalapeño pepper, deseeded and minced
½ teaspoon allspice powder
1 teaspoon salt
3 Tablespoons lemon juice
3 large Idaho potatoes, peeled and grated
3 Tablespoons canola oil
1 lemon, cut into cubes
1 teaspoon chaat masala

Method

In a large bowl, combine shrimp, ginger, garlic, cilantro, jalapeño, allspice, salt, and lemon juice. Let the shrimp marinate for 1–2 hours.

Grate the potato into longish threads. Remove the shrimp from the marinade and place it on the board. Wrap the grated potato shreds around the shrimp and place them on a plate. Wrap all the shrimp in this way until they are done.

In a large frying pan, let the oil sizzle. Now gently place the potato-crusted shrimp into the pan and fry on one side and then fry on the other side. Remove from oil and drain them on a paper towel. Squeeze lemon juice from the lemon cubes onto the shrimp and sprinkle with chaat masala.

Pineapple Shrimp

serves 4   *calories per serving: 319*   *total fat per serving: 13.0 g*

This is a simple recipe in which a small amount of chili oil is used as a bath for the shrimp before they are cooked. The assembly and the procedure are simple and take very little time. Other oils can be infused with herbs or spices and used to create entirely new dishes.

Ingredients

1 pound of shrimp, deveined and cleaned
½ teaspoon cumin powder
1 teaspoon coriander powder
½ teaspoon chaat masala
Salt to taste
1 cup pineapple cubes
3 Tablespoons lime juice
3 Tablespoons cilantro leaves

Ingredients for Chili Oil

1 cup canola oil
4–6 dry chilies

Method

In a medium-sized pot, combine canola oil and chilies. Heat the oil thoroughly, and then switch off the heat. Let the chilies steep in 1 cup of canola oil. Cool the remainder of the oil and store it in a jar.

Marinate the shrimp in 2 Tablespoons of chili oil for 1 hour. Then remove the shrimp from the marinade and dust them with cumin, coriander, chaat masala, and salt.

Skewer the shrimp, along with the pineapple. Grill the skewers. Sprinkle lime juice and cilantro on top. Serve hot.

Grilled Fish and Ginger

serves 4–6 calories per serving: 295   *total fat per serving: 19.2 g*

This is a grilled fish recipe served with a delicious lemongrass-ginger sauce. Fish and ginger have a great affinity for each other and always go well together.

Ingredients

2 large red snappers or any other firm, quality fish, scaled and cleaned
Salt and pepper to taste
1 teaspoon turmeric powder
1 teaspoon garam masala
½ teaspoon cayenne pepper
1 Tablespoon olive oil

Ingredients for Lemongrass-Ginger Sauce

1 large stalk of lemongrass, chopped finely
1 large piece of ginger, peeled and chopped finely
2 shallots, peeled and chopped finely
½ teaspoon red chili flakes
1 teaspoon olive oil
1 teaspoon tamarind paste
½ teaspoon brown sugar
½ cup basil leaves
1 lime, cut into wedges
Salt and pepper to taste

Method

Wash the fish with vinegar to remove the fishy smell. Add salt, pepper, turmeric, garam masala, and cayenne pepper. Brush the fish with olive oil and grill.

To make the lemongrass-ginger sauce, combine lemongrass, ginger, shallots, red pepper flakes, and olive oil in a mixer, and grind this into a sauce. In a small saucepan, whisk one teaspoon of olive oil to give it a good body. Add the tamarind paste and brown sugar. Then add basil leaves and remove it from heat.

Transfer the fish onto a platter, and pour the lemongrass-ginger sauce on top. Serve the fish with lime wedges and extra sauce on the side.

Mango Shrimp

serves 4   *calories per serving: 490*   *total fat per serving: 37.2 g*

This is a simple shrimp curry made with raw mango. The mango will impart a tartness to the curry. If raw mango is not available, than raw papaya can be used.

Ingredients

2 Tablespoons canola oil
2 large onions, peeled and finely chopped
½ teaspoon turmeric powder
½ teaspoon mustard seeds
6 curry leaves
1 large piece of ginger, peeled and finely chopped
1 green jalapeño chili
1 raw mango, peeled and cubed
¼ teaspoon fenugreek seeds
1 can of coconut milk
1 pound shrimp, peeled and deveined
½ bag of baby spinach leaves, chopped into thin strips
1 cup of cilantro leaves, washed and chopped coarsely
Salt and pepper to taste

Method

Heat the oil in a large saucepan. Add onions, turmeric, mustard seeds, curry leaves, ginger, and green chili.

Add mango and fenugreek seeds. Let this cook for 2 minutes or so, and add coconut milk.

Finally, add shrimp and spinach leaves, stir, and let cook for five minutes. Garnish with cilantro leaves and salt and pepper to taste.

Minty Squid Salad

serves 4   calories per serving: 212   total fat per serving: 8.8 g

This is a basic salad with mint and tamarind. Lemon juice can be substituted for tamarind. Spinach and mint are added to increase both the flavor and the visual appeal of the salad.

Ingredients

1 pound of squid rings or 5 squid whole, cleaned, and cut into rings
½ teaspoon turmeric powder
1–2 Tablespoons of olive oil
1 teaspoon red pepper flakes
1 large red onion, chopped into thin strips
1 cup mint leaves
1 cup cilantro leaves
1 lime, cut and juiced
1 teaspoon brown sugar
1 teaspoon tamarind mixed with 2 Tablespoons water
2 large tomatoes, chopped finely
1 bunch baby spinach leaves
Salt and pepper to taste

Method

Stir-fry the squid rings with turmeric powder in a Tablespoon of oil for 2 minutes.

Then put the squid in a bowl and add red pepper flakes, red onion, mint, cilantro, lime juice, olive oil, brown sugar, tamarind-water mixture, and tomatoes.

Add spinach leaves, salt, and pepper.
Toss everything lightly, and serve on a platter.

Breads and Rice Dishes

Rice and breads are used in combination with lentils and curry dishes, where the bread could be dipped in the curries. Rice is a symbol of prosperity and can be used in sweet or savory dishes. Rice is used in festive pilafs and rice salads, as well as puddings. Breads can be simple or stuffed with various ingredients, and are usually made with wheat flour or all-purpose flour. The stuffing comes in various varieties, such as lentils, herbs, vegetables, and cheese.

Quick Orzo Salad

serves 4–6   calories per serving: 400   total fat per serving: 8.5 g

Orzo salad is mixed with different herbs and spices, and infused with ginger oil. Orzo is a pasta which looks like rice, and here any other pasta or even rice can be substituted.

Ingredients

2 cups orzo, boiled al dente
1 cup grapes, chopped in half
1 orange, cut into segments
2 Tablespoons cilantro leaves, chopped finely
½ cup chopped scallions
1/3 teaspoon cumin powder
1/3 teaspoon coriander powder
A pinch of garam masala
4 Tablespoons lemon juice
Salt and pepper to taste

Ingredients for Ginger Oil

6 slices ginger, peeled
1 cup olive oil

Method

To make the ginger oil, add thin slices of ginger to hot oil, and let it steep for a few hours.
Boil the orzo in hot water and let it cook for 9–10 minutes. Drain the orzo.

In a large bowl, combine the orzo with grapes, orange segments, cilantro leaves, and scallions. Then add cumin, coriander, garam masala and lemon juice.

Add 2 Tablespoons of ginger oil; also add salt and pepper to taste.

Shrimp and Rice Salad
with Mango Vinaigrette

serves 4–6   calories per serving: 572   *total fat per serving: 11.1 g*

This is a simple rice salad made with mango vinaigrette, which imparts sweetness; various herbs are added to give a mixture of flavors. Make sure not to add too much mint, as it can be overwhelming.

Ingredients

1 pound of shrimp, peeled and deveined
¾ teaspoon salt
½ teaspoon pepper
2½ cups basmati rice, cooked
1 teaspoon cumin powder
1 Tablespoons olive oil
½ cup basil leaves, washed and chopped finely
½ cup mint leaves, washed and chopped coarsely
½ cup cilantro leaves, washed and chopped finely
¼ cup scallions, washed and chopped finely
1 cup fresh mango, chopped and cubed
2 Tablespoons toasted chopped cashews

Ingredients for Mango Vinaigrette

1 Tablespoon olive oil
1 cup mango, diced into cubes
½ teaspoon red chili flakes
1 teaspoon lemon zest

2 teaspoons lemon juice
1 cup Spanish onions, peeled and chopped finely
2 cloves garlic, peeled and minced finely
1 teaspoon cumin powder
Salt to taste

Method

Make the vinaigrette by adding all the ingredients in a mixer
and blending it. Keep it aside.

Sprinkle the shrimp with olive oil. Grill the shrimp, and then
dust it with salt and pepper. In a large bowl, combine shrimp,
cumin, rice, basil, mint, cilantro, scallions, mango, and toasted
cashews.

Add the mango vinaigrette and serve at room temperature or
cold.

Butternut Squash Rice

serves 4–6   calories per serving: 335   *total fat per serving: 7.6 g*

This simple rice recipe is made with butternut squash. Note that you can add any other squash or different vegetables. Rice is made with many different vegetables and even cheeses. The squash in this dish imparts a mild sweetness to the dish.

Ingredients

2 Tablespoons olive oil
1 butternut squash, skinned and cut into cubes
4 cups vegetable broth or water
1 cinnamon stick
3 cloves
1 large cardamom pod
1 teaspoon cumin powder
¼ cup roasted yellow split peas
½ teaspoon garam masala
Salt and pepper to taste
2 cups long-grain basmati rice
2–3 Tablespoons lemon juice
1 cup chopped mint leaves

Method

Cook the squash in water or broth until the squash is just cooked. Remove it and set aside.

To the water, add cinnamon, cloves, cardamom, cumin, garam masala, and roasted yellow split peas. Add salt and let it cook for 3 minutes. Add rice and let simmer.

Now add squash, black pepper, and lemon juice. The rice will be a little soupy. Garnish it with mint leaves, and serve with lemon slices.

Fragrant Herbed Rice

serves 4–6   calories per serving: 274   total fat per serving: 3.0 g

In this delicious dish, fragrant basmati rice is mixed with herbs to create a savory side dish. You can also add any green leafy vegetables, if desired. This rice can go with meat dishes as well as vegetarian fare.

Ingredients

4 cups of cooked, plain, long-grain basmati rice
1 Tablespoon extra virgin olive oil
¼ cup fresh lemon juice
2 cups cilantro leaves, washed and chopped coarsely
1 cup mint leaves, chopped finely
10 sprigs of curry leaves, chopped finely
½ cup scallions, chopped finely
1-inch piece of ginger, grated finely
4 large tomatoes, cored, seeded, and chopped into cubes
½ teaspoon red pepper flakes
Salt and pepper to taste

Method

Put the cooked rice in a large bowl. Add all the listed ingredients to the rice.
Add salt and pepper to taste. Serve cold as a salad.

Shrimp Pilaf

serves 4–6   calories per serving: 558   total fat per serving: 9.4 g

This is a basic prawn pilaf made with shiitake mushrooms and peas. Use vegetables that are not strong in flavor so that the vegetables take on the flavors of the prawns and spices. Shrimp pilaf can be a main course with yogurt and a vegetable side dish.

Ingredients

1 cup medium-sized shrimp, deveined and cleaned
1 large piece of ginger, peeled and minced into a paste
2 cloves of garlic, peeled and minced
1 jalapeño pepper, deseeded and minced
1 cup cilantro leaves, washed and chopped coarsely
2 Tablespoons of canola oil
4 Tablespoons of lemon juice
1 large red onion, peeled and chopped finely
1 bay leaf
½ teaspoon cayenne pepper
¾ teaspoon turmeric powder
2 cups basmati rice, washed and drained
1 pound shiitake mushrooms
1 cup frozen green peas, thawed and drained
4 cups chicken broth
Salt to taste
1 teaspoon freshly ground pepper

Method

Marinate the shrimp with ginger, garlic, jalapeño, ½ cup cilantro, and 1 Tablespoon of lemon juice. Marinate for about 3 hours or so.

In a large pot, pour canola oil. Add onions, bay leaf, cayenne pepper, and turmeric. Let it cook for 2 minutes or so on medium heat. Add shrimp and rice, and sauté everything in the pot. Add shiitake mushrooms, peas, and chicken broth. Cover and cook on a low heat.

After the rice is done, add remaining cilantro leaves and lemon juice; salt and pepper to taste.

Barley Risotto

serves 4   *calories per serving: 309*   *total fat per serving: 3.2 g*

This is made in the style of a risotto, and the grains are not separated but are lumped together. It can be served as a savory side or even as a breakfast food. Barley is a healthy choice in place of rice or pasta.

Ingredients

2 cups pearl barley
1 Tablespoon olive oil
1 yellow onion chopped finely
4 cups water
1 cup raisins (or more, if you like it sweet)
3–4 Tablespoons lemon juice
Salt and pepper to taste
1 cup parsley leaves, chopped coarsely
¼ teaspoon cayenne pepper
¼ teaspoon chaat masala
1 teaspoon honey

Method

Rinse the barley a few times to remove any impurities.
In a large pan, combine oil, barley, and onion, and let it cook.
Let the barley fry until it turns brown and nutty.
Add 4 cups water to the barley and let it cook on a low heat until the barley absorbs all the water. (If it looks dry, add more water.)

Transfer it to a bowl. Add raisins, lemon juice, salt, pepper, parsley, cayenne, and chaat masala.

Add a drizzle of honey on top of the barley and mix until well blended. Serve at room temperature.

Fast Chicken Pilaf

serves 4   *calories per serving: 490*   *total fat per serving: 8.4 g*

This is a simple pilaf recipe made with chicken. If you do not like the nuts, they may be omitted. It is a quick recipe and can be whipped up in a short amount of time. Basically, it is rice and chicken put together to create a quick easy dish.

Ingredients

2 Tablespoon canola oil
2 cups long-grain basmati rice
2 teaspoons of milk
½ teaspoon saffron threads
2 large boneless chicken breasts, cut into medium-sized pieces
1 teaspoon cardamom powder
1 teaspoon cinnamon powder
1 teaspoon clove powder
Salt and pepper to taste
1 cup nonfat yogurt
1 teaspoon paprika powder
1 cinnamon stick
2 bay leaves
1 Tablespoon tomato paste
4 cups of water
2 teaspoons of almonds, slivered

Method

Rinse the rice and let it steep in water for 15 minutes; drain.

In a small bowl, pour 2 teaspoons of milk. Add saffron threads and steep them in the milk for 15 minutes or so.

In a large bowl, add chicken, cardamom, cinnamon powder, clove powder, salt, and a few grinds of pepper. Add yogurt, mix the chicken well, and keep aside for 1–2 hours.

In a large pot, combine 2 Tablespoons canola oil, cinnamon stick, bay leaves, tomato paste, paprika, and the chicken mixture. Cook all this for a few minutes. Now transfer the washed rice to the pot and let the rice fry along with the spices. Add 4 cups water and let everything cook until the rice is done.

When the rice is almost done, add the saffron steeped in milk. Garnish with almonds and serve.

Red Pepper and Basil Pilaf

serves 4   *calories per serving: 375*   *total fat per serving: 4.1 g*

This is a basic pilaf in which red pepper is roasted and combined with basil. If you wish to substitute for red pepper, you can use yellow pepper since these peppers both have a mild, sweetish taste. Store-bought roasted peppers can be used to save on time and effort. Any other combination of herb and vegetable can be used to make your own delicious recipe.

Ingredients

1 Tablespoon olive oil
2 large yellow onions
2 garlic cloves, peeled and minced finely
1 roasted red bell peppers, chopped into pieces
1 cinnamon stick
2 bay leaves
A pinch of sugar
3 green cardamoms crushed lightly
2 cups basmati rice
4 cups of water
2 cups basil leaves chopped into thin strips
1 Tablespoon lemon zest
Salt and pepper to taste

Method

In a medium-sized vessel, combine olive oil, onions, and garlic. Sauté the onions and garlic until they turn golden brown. Add roasted red peppers, cinnamon stick, bay leaves, sugar, and cardamom pods. Let this cook for 5 minutes. Add the rice to the pot, and sauté it for a few minutes until well coated with olive oil. Add 4 cups of water and let it cook on low heat until it is done. Add salt and pepper.

Add the thin strips of basil leaves and lemon zest, and serve.

Cheese and Mint Bread

serves 6   *calories per serving: 265*   *total fat per serving: 9.6 g*

This is bread that is stuffed with the unusual combination of goat cheese and mint leaves. The goat cheese imparts a tangy flavor, and the mint brings freshness to the bread. This bread can be eaten at breakfast as well as a snack.

Ingredients

2 cups whole wheat flour
1 Tablespoon canola oil
½ teaspoon salt
1 teaspoon pepper
4 ounces of goat cheese
1 bunch mint leaves, chopped finely

Method

Pour the flour in a nonreactive bowl. Make a well in the middle of the flour and add oil, salt, and pepper. Add a few spoons of water and work the flour and all the ingredients to make pliable dough.

Extract a small ball of dough, make it into a bowl shape, and fill it with the mint and goat cheese. Close the bowl by bringing in the sides of the dough and covering the goat cheese and mint mixture. Gently roll out the flat bread and pan-fry them on a griddle. Serve hot.

Jalapeño Cheese Bread

serves 6   calories per serving: 252   total fat per serving: 9.1 g

This is a cheese bread with jalapeño added to spice it up. You can substitute any cheese of your liking. Breads are eaten very often with vegetables and curries. This is a variation on a bread recipe with extra zing added to the bread.

Ingredients

2 cups whole wheat flour
½ cup all-purpose flour
1 teaspoon grated ginger
1 teaspoon chaat masala
1 teaspoon cumin seeds
1 teaspoon garam masala
Salt and pepper to taste
A pinch of cayenne pepper
1–2 cups grated Monterey Jack cheese
1–2 jalapeño peppers, finely chopped
½ cup cilantro leaves, finely chopped
1 Tablespoon canola oil

Method

In a large bowl, combine flours, ginger, chaat masala, cumin seeds, garam masala, salt, pepper, and a pinch of cayenne pepper. Make a well and add oil. Now work the dough to create a ball. Cover it with a damp towel and let it rest.

Make a mixture of grated cheese and minced jalapeño peppers

and cilantro leaves.

Now pinch small pieces of the dough and roll them into discs of about 3 inches. Then add the jalapeño cheese mixture to the middle of the disc. Now cover the cheese mixture with the dough on the side to form a ball. Roll the bread into a 6–8-inch disc. Put the bread on a pan. Cook the bread on one side, then flip and cook on the other side. Make all the breads this way. Add a few drops of olive oil on top of each disc when done.

Sweet Stuffed Banana Bread

serves 4–6   calories per serving: 327   total fat per serving: 4.4 g

In this unique dish, bananas are mashed into a pulp and used as a stuffing for the bread. This bread is both sweet and spicy. It can be eaten at breakfast or used as a snack with tea.

Ingredients

1 Tablespoon canola oil
2 cups whole wheat flour
2 ripe bananas, mashed into a pulp
1 teaspoon cardamom powder
1 Tablespoon lemon juice
1 Tablespoon sugar
4 Tablespoons sweet coconut flakes
1 teaspoon ground white pepper
Salt to taste

Method

In a large bowl, combine oil, flour, mashed bananas, cardamom, lemon juice, sugar, coconut flakes, white pepper, and salt. Work the dough to create a ball. Cover it with a damp towel and let the dough rest for 30 minutes.

Take small pinches of the dough and roll them into 6-inch discs.

Sprinkle a few drops of oil in a pan, and insert the bread gently into the pan. Cook the bread on one side; then flip and cook on the other side. Serve warm.

Sweet Little Things

Indian desserts are delicious and often presented in an elaborate manner. Sweets are largely milk-based and often contain vegetables like carrot or pumpkin, as well as fruits like mangoes and bananas. Different flours, like rice flour and chickpea flour, are used to make different varieties of sweets. No Indian meal is complete or fulfilling without an enticing dessert.

Mango Crème Brulée

serves 4   calories per serving: 288   total fat per serving: 4.9 g

Crème brulée is a classic dessert that is a downright winner. Here, it is made with mango, milk, and cream to produce a delectable dessert. Cinnamon, nutmeg, clove, and cardamom enhance the basic flavors of mango and cream.

Ingredients

2½ cups milk
1 can mango pulp
¼ teaspoon nutmeg
A pinch of clove powder
½ teaspoon ginger powder
4 eggs
½ cup Splenda sugar substitute
1 teaspoon cardamom powder

Method

Boil milk and mango pulp. Add nutmeg, clove powder, and ginger. Cool this mixture.

In another bowl, beat 4 eggs, along with Splenda. Beat thoroughly. Add the cooled milk mixture to the egg-Splenda mixture. Pour into the crème brulée cups. Put them in a water bath. Bake at 300 degrees for 30 minutes.

Remove and chill the crème brulée. When about to serve, add Splenda and cardamom powder on top, and place it under a broiler until the Splenda melts.

Pink Raspberry Pudding

serves 6   *calories per serving: 159*   *total fat per serving: 4.9 g*

This is very much a pudding recipe made with raspberries. Any fruit, especially berries, will be delicious. It is often served cold and is splendid in summer months.

Ingredients

3 Tablespoons long-grain rice
1 pint of raspberries, washed
½ cup water
¾ cup Splenda sugar substitute
6 cups milk
10 pistachios nuts, chopped into small bits
1 teaspoon cardamom powder

Method

Soak the rice for 2 hours. Drain the water and grind the rice to a coarse paste.

In a blender, combine half the raspberries, ½ cup water, and half of the sugar substitute, and blend into a puree.

Mix the raspberry puree and ground rice together. Set aside.

Bring the milk to a boil in a large pot. Stir the raspberry-rice puree into the milk. Stir the remaining sugar substitute into the milk until the sugar completely dissolves.

Pour this mixture into nice ceramic bowls. Garnish it with pistachios and remaining raspberries, and dust it with cardamom powder. Serve chilled.

Mango Tart

serves 6   calories per serving: 291   total fat per serving: 8.7 g

This simple tart is made with mangoes, but fruits such as apples, peaches, or pears can be used instead. Tart is a new invention in modern Indian cuisine. Here, mango is used to flavor the tart.

Ingredients for Shell

1 store-bought pie pastry
1 medium-sized egg, slightly beaten

Ingredients for Filling

1 package of mascarpone cheese
½ cup Splenda sugar substitute
½ teaspoon vanilla extract
1 Tablespoon chopped pistachios
1 teaspoon cardamom powder
2 ripe mangoes, cut into cubes

Method

Roll the pastry sheet on a floured pastry board to ⅛-inch thickness. Drape it over rolling pin and transfer it to a 10-inch fluted flan tin with a removable bottom. Be careful not to stretch it. Squeeze the dough inside the pan so that no air bubbles remain. Roll the rolling pin across the top of the ring to trim the excess dough. Reform the edges and crimp. Brush the pastry shell with egg.

Prick shell on the bottom and cover it with foil paper to ensure the sheet doesn't rise unevenly. Fill it and bake it with any type of beans or even rice. Bake it on the on the lowermost rack of the oven at 400 degrees for 15 minutes or until slightly golden brown. Place on a wire rack to cool.

To make the filling, combine ingredients in a food processor and puree. Pour the mixture into the pie shell and bake at 375 degrees for 20 minutes or until the top sets at the edges.

Remove the tart from the fluted ring and sprinkle it with chopped pistachios and cardamom powder. Serve with vanilla ice cream.

Yogurt Mousse with Pineapple

serves 4–6   calories per serving: 63   total fat per serving: 0.8 g

This is a low-calorie dessert made with nonfat yogurt. Any other fruit, such as mangoes or peaches, can be substituted for pineapple. The yogurt and the fruit mixed together make for a luscious dessert.

Ingredients

1 jar nonfat yogurt about 35 oz
1 can pineapple slices, chopped finely
1 Tablespoon honey
½ teaspoon saffron threads
1 Tablespoon warm milk
1 teaspoon cardamom powder

Method

Transfer yogurt into a bowl. Strain the yogurt to remove all the water by putting the yogurt in a cheese cloth. Add honey to the yogurt. Chop the pineapple slices and pass them through a small food processor.
Soak the saffron threads in 1 Tablespoon warm milk. Let the saffron steep well.
In a large decorative bowl, combine yogurt, pureed pineapple, saffron milk, and cardamom powder. Serve cold.

Vanilla Vermicelli Pudding

serves 6   *calories per serving: 280*   *total fat per serving: 6.0 g*

This is a basic vermicelli pudding to which vanilla is added to give it a twist. Milk pudding is popular and is also made with rice or flaked rice or even tapioca pearls. Here vermicelli is used and flavored with vanilla bean.

Ingredients

1 Tablespoon canola oil
2 cups vermicelli, broken into pieces
4 cups milk
1½ cups Splenda sugar substitute
1 vanilla bean
1 teaspoon cardamom powder
2 teaspoons almond or cashew powder
½ teaspoon saffron threads
2 teaspoons chopped pistachios

Method

In a medium-sized pan, combine oil and vermicelli, and fry until it becomes golden brown.

In a Dutch oven, pour the milk and sugar and stir until the sugar dissolves.

Transfer the vanilla bean (slit apart) into the milk and let it steep for a while. Add the sautéed vermicelli into the milk, along with cardamom powder and almond or cashew powder. Add saffron threads to the mixture. Let it cook until the milk slightly thickens.

Cool the pudding and refrigerate it to chill. Serve it in bowls and top it with chopped pistachios.

Sweet Saffron Pudding

serves 6   calories per serving: 313   total fat per serving: 6.1 g

This is an excellent dish made with Cream of Wheat and flavored with saffron and cardamom. This dessert has few ingredients, but the end result is wonderful.

Ingredients

4 cups whole milk
1½ cups Splenda sugar substitute
1 Tablespoon saffron threads
1 Tablespoon clarified butter
1 Tablespoon canola oil
2 cups Cream of Wheat
1 Tablespoon cardamom powder
1 Tablespoon sliced almonds

Method

In a medium-sized pot, combine milk, Splenda, and saffron. Let the saffron steep in the milk for 10 minutes and let the milk boil slowly until the Splenda dissolves and the milk is slightly reduced and becomes somewhat thick.

In another pan, fry the Cream of Wheat, the clarified butter, and the oil on a low heat. The Cream of Wheat will turn a brownish color and will exude a roasted aroma.

Transfer the roasted Cream of Wheat into the milk. Now cook the roasted Cream of Wheat in milk on a low heat. Stir vigorously until the Cream of Wheat starts to thicken and absorb the milk with saffron and sugar. Add cardamom powder and sliced almonds.

This sweet saffron pudding is delicious served hot or cold.

Ricotta Cheese Squares

serves 4–6   calories per serving: 462   total fat per serving: 15.1 g

In this recipe, the milk, sugar, and ricotta cheese are combined to create a sumptuous dessert. The milk is boiled and reduced until it becomes thick and is flavored with rose essence.

Ingredients

4 cups ricotta cheese
1½ cups Splenda sugar substitute
4 cups 1% milk
1 teaspoon cardamom powder
1 teaspoon rose water

Method

In a large bowl, combine ricotta and 1 cup Splenda, and blend this in a mixer. Transfer this into a baking dish and bake for 40 minutes at 350 degrees. In a saucepan, boil milk and remaining ½ cup Splenda on a low heat until it thickens. Add cardamom powder and rose water.

After 40 minutes, remove the baked ricotta from the oven. Cool it and cut into squares. Pour the milk into a large baking dish. Add the ricotta squares to the milk and chill in the refrigerator. Serve cold.

Royal Bread Pudding

serves 6   calories per serving: 345   total fat per serving: 11.3 g

Bread pudding is a comfort food, and it is good on warm summer days. This dessert is served cold.

Ingredients

8 slices of white sandwich bread
4 Tablespoons canola oil
1 quart 1% milk
1 cup Splenda sugar substitute
1 teaspoon vanilla extract
1 Tablespoon ground cardamom powder

Method

Cut the crusts off the bread and cut bread in half diagonally. Each slice should yield 2 triangles.
Pour the oil in a frying pan, and fry the triangles. Drain the oil off the bread and keep them on a paper towel.
In another large saucepan, combine milk and Splenda and heat it on low. The milk should reduce and become slightly thick. Cool the milk and add vanilla.
Transfer the bread slices into a deep baking dish, stacking two triangles together. Pour the thickened, cooled milk over them. Add ground cardamom powder.
Refrigerate the dessert and serve it chilled.

Banana Coconut Dumplings

serves 6   calories per serving: 342   total fat per serving: 12.5 g

Dumplings are simple to make and tasty to eat. Here, phyllo sheets are used to save the time and effort of making the shell. Coconut is flavored with raisins, cardamom, sugar, and banana, and baked to produce a superbly flavorful dumpling.

Ingredients

2 ripe bananas
½ cup sweetened coconut flakes
2 teaspoons raisins
1 Tablespoon cardamom powder
Salt to taste
12 phyllo sheets
4 Tablespoons canola oil

Method

In a large bowl, mash the bananas, and add coconut, raisins, cardamom, and salt.

Lay the phyllo sheets on a cutting board and oil each sheet with canola oil. Cut the phyllo sheets in square shaped sizes and fill them with the banana-coconut mixture. Do not overfill. Gently close each packet using a bit of oil around the edges, and make it into a pouch.

Bake the dumplings at 350 degrees for 10 to 12 minutes. Remove the dumplings from the oven and let it cool for 10 minutes. Transfer the dumplings onto a plate lined with a

paper towel.
Serve with ice cream.